THE
HIDDEN
HISTORY
of
CHESTER
COUNTY

*Lost Tales from the
Delaware & Brandywine Valleys*

—◆—

MARK E. DIXON

THE
History
PRESS

Published by The History Press
Charleston, SC 29403
www.historypress.net

Cover images: Sharples Separator ad courtesy of the Chester County Historical Society. Fox hunting and photography images courtesy of the Library of Congress.

First published 2011

Manufactured in the United States

ISBN 978.1.60949.073.7

Library of Congress Cataloging-in-Publication Data

Dixon, Mark E.
The hidden history of Chester County : lost tales from the Delaware and Brandywine
Valleys / Mark Dixon.
p. cm.
Includes bibliographical references.
ISBN 978-1-60949-073-7
1. Chester County (Pa.)--History--Anecdotes. 2. Chester County (Pa.)--History, Local-
-Anecdotes. 3. Chester County (Pa.)--Biography--Anecdotes. 4. Chester County (Pa.)--
Social life and customs--Anecdotes. I. Title.
F157.C4D594 2011
974.8'13--dc22
2011003671

CONTENTS

CONTENTS

FOREWORD

Chester County's been around for more than three hundred years. Established by William Penn in 1682 as one of the three original counties of Pennsylvania (Philadelphia and Bucks being the other two), Chester County started out really big and still is, even after Lancaster County was carved off from the west in 1729 and Delaware County from the southeast in 1789. Penn's promise of religious tolerance convinced many to make the decision to leave their homes, cross the Atlantic and settle in Pennsylvania. Early years saw the arrival of settlers of various religious denominations looking for a place where they could practice their faith in peace. They would be joined by those seeking opportunity and hoping for a fresh start.

How to address these three hundred years of history can be a daunting task. One of the best ways to make history compelling is to tell stories about individuals. Mark Dixon is a gifted storyteller who can craft a narrative that is both informative and entertaining. Although we may be centuries removed from those who preceded us, Dixon shows us that we are not as different as we might think. He is also not afraid to express a point of view.

Dixon's latest book, *The Hidden History of Chester County*, is filled with stories about people that illustrate the best and worst of human nature. Nathan Evans wouldn't stop speaking up about the evils of slavery. A long-buried local hero is disinterred to promote a new cemetery. A determined politician sticks to his beliefs as his own party pressures him to conform. Ann Preston perseveres and establishes the Women's Hospital of Philadelphia in 1862. A decade later, William Eachus Udderzook and his brother-in-law concoct an insurance fraud scheme that eventually leads to murder. A much honored marine speaks his mind and gets court-martialed.

Many of these are tales of lasting, significant contributions to society, and others are stories about what we might consider the more idiosyncratic (and entertaining) footnotes of history—such as the Battle Axes. (Really? A free love cult in northern Chester County? In the 1840s?)

For those who think that they have a pretty good handle on the history of Chester County, prepare to raise an eyebrow or two. If the county is new to you, welcome! There are a lot of stories hidden in those three centuries.

Diane P. Rofini
Librarian
Chester County Historical Society

ACKNOWLEDGEMENTS

Having been preceded by similar books of stories about the Main Line and Delaware County, this book of Chester County stories is the last (for a while) and, therefore, also my last opportunity to thank those who have helped along the way.

Special thanks to *Main Line Today* magazine, which originally published these stories, and to its editor, Hobart Rowland. The magazine has given me an unusual opportunity, which I very much appreciate. How many magazines of its type make room among the restaurant reviews and house-remodeling features for stories about dead people? For his part, Hobart has remained consistently broad-minded about my subject matter and tolerant of my flexible interpretation of deadlines. (Don't ever change, Hobart.)

Thanks also to my wife, Cynthia, and daughters, Abigail and Rachel, for listening to many of these stories and tolerating my strange hours. Rachel? Thumbs up to you for sitting there quietly with your homework when I have to drag you along to some weird library with no tween books. You rock.

And here's the part I dread: no more opportunities to thank my helpful friends. Previously, I could thank people "in my next book." Now, at the end of this three-part series, anyone I forget now may go perpetually unthanked. It's a shame and I apologize. Really, folks, it's not you. It's me.

Again, thanks.

1705

WHEN PACIFISTS LIVED DANGEROUSLY

Pacifists are cowards. Everyone "knows" that. But then, few have witnessed a real pacifist—say, John Smith (1681–1766) of London Grove—in action.

Smith, who came to Pennsylvania when pacifists were still in charge, was not a conscientious objector. That's a Selective Service category invented for people who have been granted official permission to be pacifists. Smith—whose bravery shamed those who insisted that he fight—didn't ask permission.

Born in Dartmouth, Massachusetts, Smith was the grandson of English immigrants. There had been soldiers in the family. His mother's father had been killed in 1676 fighting the Narragansett Indians in King Philip's War. His father's father, Lieutenant John Smith, had been the chief military officer of Dartmouth. However, Smith's parents, Eleazer and Ruth, had fallen in with the Quakers, and it was that religion to which Smith would later point.

In 1700, a long way from Massachusetts, the childless king of Spain, Charles II, died. Charles left his throne to a grandson of the king of France. This was too close to a merger of Spain and France to suit other European powers—especially Great Britain, which feared the two countries' united military and economic muscle. England and its allies insisted that the Spanish throne go to another heir. That was refused, leading to the War of the Spanish Succession, which lasted thirteen years, accomplished little and killed at least 100,000 people.

This was relevant to Smith because London soon instructed its American colonies to join the conflict by attacking French colonies in Canada.

In 1703, Colonel Benjamin Church—who had an established reputation for killing both Indians and French settlers—was assembling an expedition

Quaker pacifist John Smith of Dartmouth, Massachusetts, refused to take part in a 1704 attack on the original version of this reconstructed fort at Port Royal, Nova Scotia. It was the start of what Smith—who later migrated to Chester County—called becoming "acquainted with the discipline of the cross." *Danielle Langlois.*

to what is now New Brunswick and Nova Scotia. Church needed men, of course. In August, Corporal William Hart knocked on John Smith's door. Be at the town hall on such and such a day to be mustered into the militia, he told the twenty-one-year-old. But when the day arrived, Smith did not go.

It was the beginning of the time, Smith later wrote, when he "came to be acquainted with the discipline of the cross."

Summoned to court, Smith was fined six pounds, three shillings. He refused to pay. Quakers believed that Christians didn't pay for the privilege of obeying the Lord's commandments.

The court threw Smith in jail for a month. He still refused to pay. Next the court offered to sell Smith as an indentured servant for four years to anyone who would pay the fine. No one came forward. (Smith must have seemed an unpromising servant.) Two weeks later, Smith was tossed aboard a boat bound for Boston where, it was believed, the military was equipped to deal with him.

While sailing around Cape Cod, however, Smith saved the ship when a squall laid the lightly ballasted vessel on its side. "I ran and loosed the sails so that she got righted before any of the hands on board came to my assistance which [they] seeing were glad of my company," he wrote. Smith arrived in Boston a hero and with new respect that he hadn't felt when everyone considered him a simple malingerer.

"The people [now] behaved civilly towards me, as believing I acted from a religious principle," he wrote. "But finding they could not make me submit to them, they set me at liberty." (Even so, he spent four months locked up in the fort.)

That wasn't the end of it. In the spring of 1705, Smith sailed as a common seaman aboard a merchant ship bound for London. Eight weeks later, the ship sailed into the harbor at Plymouth, England, where seventeen British

Never popular in any era, pacifists infuriated Theodore Roosevelt, who was eager to get into World War I. Said Roosevelt, "The pacifist is as surely a traitor to his country and to humanity as is the most brutal wrongdoer." *Library of Congress.*

warships lay at anchor. One sent aboard a press gang that brought back Smith and another Quaker, Thomas Anthony, who probably appeared to be likely recruits for Her Majesty's navy.

The next day, when the warship lifted anchor, Smith and Anthony were ordered to help sail it. They refused, though a lieutenant "swore divers times he would run us through with his sword." Soon, an enemy warship was sighted off the coast of France, and all around sailors ran to their battle stations.

"They placed us to a gun and commanded us to fight," said Smith. "But we told them we would not, for Christ and his apostles spake to the contrary." In the heat of battle, Smith and Anthony were apparently pushed aside and, for several days, forgotten.

In the seventeenth-century British navy, sailors spent most of their time below deck unless required above. But one day, as Smith sat below decks waiting for orders to refuse, he felt a "calling" to go topside. Twice he went up and twice he came back, "growing very uneasy; it was said in the secret of my heart [that] 'thou knowest where to get relief.'" He went up a third time and was seen from the quarterdeck by a lieutenant who asked the boatswain if he had made the Quaker work yet. Hearing that he had not, the lieutenant handed the boatswain his cane and ordered him to beat Smith until he complied.

"Then the boatswain took the cane and laid on my head with such violence that he beat my hat to pieces," said Smith, who still refused to work. Next, the lieutenant ordered Smith tied to the gears, the mechanism used to raise and lower the anchor. What followed—a whipping on Smith's bare back with the cat-o'-nine-tails—was like a scene from *Mutiny on the Bounty*, though with a twist not seen in the movies.

"On my knees, it arose in my mind to pray for my persecutors for they knew not what they did," wrote Smith.

Put yourself in the place of the boatswain, the lieutenant or any sailor who witnessed this scene. You've bought the recruiter's myth and joined the navy to serve queen and country. Now, here you are, whipping a defenseless fellow Englishman as he kneels in his own blood, praying for your soul. It could only cause shame.

"True pacifism," said Reverend Martin Luther King Jr., who led unarmed demonstrators against violent opposition, shows that it is better to be the target than the one who inflicts violence. In the process, he said, pacifism "may develop a sense of shame in the opponent, and thereby bring about a transformation and change of heart."

Years later, Smith wrote that "through the Lord's mercy, they were not suffered to strike me any more." Moreover, his courage seems to have touched the crew. The boatswain's mate took Smith by the shoulder and "asked why [he] did not stay below decks," adding, "You have been beat enough to kill an ox."

In September 1705, the ship again dropped anchor in Plymouth harbor, where the captain gave Smith and Anthony one final order. "Since we were not men for his purpose," wrote Smith, "the captain said he gave us leave to go on shore, but said nothing of our coming on board again." They obeyed this order to its letter, though Anthony—who had also been viciously beaten—died of his injuries not long after.

English Quakers provided passage to Pennsylvania, where, in 1707, Smith married Ann, a daughter of Caleb Pusey, who had built William Penn's mill at Upland. The Smiths later settled in London Grove Township, where they built a stone house that still stands and helped to found the local Quaker meeting, which still exists. Sometime during Smith's long life, he set down his story—*A Narrative of Some Sufferings for His Christian Peaceable Testimony, by John Smith, late of Chester County, deceased*—published in 1800.

The last contemporary mention of Smith was in 1764, when he stood up at a Quaker gathering in Philadelphia to deplore the spread among increasingly affluent members of such customs as wearing expensive clothes, buying "fashionable" furniture and carrying silver watches.

Okay, so you may not think much of pacifists. Many people don't. But you can't call John Smith a coward.

1782

WORKING HARDER

In most human relationships, some people work harder than others. Richard Barnard (1726–1813) seems to have been one of those people. At least, he tried harder than his friend, Isaac Baily (1728–1806), who seems to have been a piece of work.

Barnard and Baily were Quaker farmers who lived on either side of Pocopson Creek in East Marlborough Township. Sometime in the late 1770s, the two men began to feud over their property line. Arbitration with other Quakers didn't resolve the issue or warm the frostiness that crept into their relationship. Barnard's solution? On a spring morning, he went to his annoying neighbor's house, knelt and washed Baily's feet.

An unsigned 1831 Quaker-published text describes the episode:

> *An evident change now took place in his neighbour's disposition, and Richard left him to his own reflections. That same day, [Barnard] observed his neighbour, with a shovel, opening the water-course, where it should run; and in the afternoon, he and his wife came over and made Richard and family a friendly social visit, manifesting an entirely different disposition from what he had indulged towards him, for several years before: for he was now open, neighbourly, and friendly, as formerly, and continued so the remainder of his days.*

Barnard and Baily were the grandsons of immigrants who had arrived with William Penn. Barnard's father, Richard Sr., had come to Marlborough in about 1715, when he bought 625 acres of land. When Baily's grandfather,

Because Richard Barnard worked a bit harder than his friend, Isaac Baily, both now lie in the burial ground of the Kennett Square's Marlborough Friends Meeting. *Mark E. Dixon.*

Joel, arrived about ten years later, he bought half of the Barnard property, which he bequeathed to his son, Isaac Sr. Upon their fathers' deaths, the two farms passed to Isaac and Richard, respectively.

During the Revolutionary War, Barnard—as was expected of all observant Quakers—refused to pay taxes to support the war. Nevertheless, he paid many times over. In 1777, detachments from the British and American armies arrived two days apart and helped themselves, respectively, to one of Barnard's horses and a wagon. In 1779, Barnard submitted peacefully when the Americans took three wagon loads of hay and corn and then returned with seventy-two army horses, which they fed for two weeks on his hay. Steers and milk cows were also seized.

Barnard didn't get credit for any of this with Joseph Luckey, the local tax collector. On Christmas Day 1780, when Barnard was absent, Luckey came to the farm and took a horse, twenty pounds of tallow, a saddle and bridle and Barnard's wallet containing two pounds and six shillings. In 1781, Luckey returned for two hogsheads of cider, a brass kettle, a steer, two heifers, forty-three bushels of wheat and a clock worth sixteen pounds—all in payment for a six-pound war tax.

At the same time, Barnard's surviving daybooks indicate that he was serving on a committee whose assignment it was to visit the few remaining Quaker slave owners and convince them to free their slaves. It was tedious and time-consuming work. Barnard must have been a patient soul—or possibly he felt a dissonance in speaking of peace to the soldiers and tax collectors when he couldn't even get along with his neighbor.

In contrast, Baily—"not so much imbued with Friendly ideas," according to a family history—was an enthusiastic supporter of the Revolution. In 1779, Kennett Quaker Meeting recorded that Baily "has paid a part of ye Bounty for ye encouragement of a Waggon & Horses to go in ye military service." In 1783, the meeting complained that Isaac had paid to hire a man to fight in his place. For Quakers, the problem with adhering to church teaching was that doing so brought heavy fines and confiscation of property by the government. Isaac apologized for his misconduct both times. An apology was necessary to avoid being expelled, though he probably wasn't very sorry.

About 1779, Baily decided to dam Pocopson Creek, which was also the property line between Barnard and himself. Why he did so was not recorded, nor is the impact on Barnard clear. The dam may have made it more difficult for Barnard to irrigate his crops, or it may have simply flooded part of his land. What is clear is that Barnard complained and got nowhere.

Baily was a child of his father's 1728 marriage to a widow with three children. Abigail Wickersham Baily had three more children with Isaac Baily Sr. and, after his death in 1732, married again and had three more. Perhaps, with two siblings and six half-siblings competing for their inheritances, young Isaac developed an exquisite sensitivity to his property rights.

In the spring of 1782, Barnard told the story to a traveling minister. The man replied simply, "Richard, there is more required of some, than of others."

But what?

"This excited in his mind a further inquiry," according to the 1831 account.

> *What could be possibly done that would be likely to have the desired effect? While in this thoughtful and inquiring state of mind, it presented to him, that he must go and wash his neighbor's feet; and he would then be friendly with him again.*
>
> *When this impression was first made, he revolted at the idea, and thought he could not do it; but the impression remained so forcibly on his mind, that after a considerable time, he became prepared to yield to it, and his eyes burst into a flood of tears.*

Among Christians, the washing of feet is inspired by the actions of Jesus at the Last Supper, when he washed his disciples' feet to demonstrate that they must abandon pride, as noted John 13:14–15: "If I then, your Lord and Master, have washed your feet; ye also ought to wash one another's feet. For I have given you an example, that ye should do as I have done to you."

However, the lesson only makes sense in the context of Christianity's origins in the ancient Middle East, where people wore sandals to walk the dusty roads and truly needed to wash their feet after a journey. At home, most people washed their own feet. But in someone else's home, the washing of guests' feet was recognized as a duty of courtesy—a mint-on-the-pillow thing. The washing itself, however, was a McJob—something delegated to the lowliest servant in the household. The task offered little compensation, not much hope for advancement and degradation in both its body language (one had to kneel to do it) and its proximity to whatever got tracked in.

Because Jesus did it, though, feet washing became a symbolic Christian ritual that has continued to the present. In the sixth century, the "father of monasticism," St. Benedict of Nursia, directed that the Maundy service—from "mandatum" (Latin for "command") in memory of Jesus's order—should be performed every Saturday for all monastery residents by whichever monk had cooking duties that week. The abbot and brethren were also to wash the feet of guests. As late as the time of Saint Bernard of Clairvaux (1090–1153), religious writers referred to feet washing as a sacrament.

However, the custom also seems to have become more ritualistic and less widely observed. In AD 300, a council of bishops meeting in Spain directed that the feet of those about to be baptized should not be washed by priests but rather by people in lesser positions. (There went the ritual's democratic implications.) In 694, the Seventeenth Synod of Toledo commanded all bishops and priests under pain of excommunication to wash the feet of those subject to them. If the hierarchy was forced to insist so strongly, it is likely that at least some clergy had ceased observing the ritual.

Most of the sovereigns of Europe used to symbolically wash the feet of several subjects on Maundy Thursday before Easter. The custom persists in Spain, but English royalty haven't washed feet since James II ended the practice in the 1680s. Since coming to the throne in 1952, Queen Elizabeth II has handed out specially minted Maundy coins to a select group of Britons aged seventy and up.

Today, feet washing is practiced by a variety of Christian denominations. Catholics and many Protestant groups observe the feast of the Lord's Supper, at which members and sometimes clergy wash one another's feet. The Baptists do it. Some Mennonites do it. In 2003, at Gloucester Cathedral, the archbishop of Canterbury washed the feet of twelve selected parishioners, including the choirmaster's teenage daughter, who washed them herself before the ceremony.

Quakers, however, never engaged in feet washing. Wary of what they considered empty symbolism and dead rituals, Quakers early in their history abolished practices such as water baptism, rote prayers, the Lord's Supper and feet washing.

However Barnard conceived the idea, what he contemplated was not the safe, ceremonial feet washing practiced on special occasions by people who liked one another, were friendly and who had prewashed their feet. The perennially cranky Baily could easily spurn him, chase him off the property and then ridicule him in the neighborhood for his weird notion.

The account continues. Barnard "arose very early in the morning…and went to his neighbour's house…and informed him that he had brought two bottles of water with him, with which he was willing to wash his feet, in that they might in future be friendly, and live as Friends should do beside each other."

Baily's immediate response was not encouraging:

> *His neighbour, at first, appeared unfriendly, and refused to let him wash his feet. Richard informed him he was entirely willing to do it, for the sake of his friendship and good will, and that he had long been distressed, when he reflected upon the manner in which they lived by each other. But he was in hopes his mind would be somewhat relieved; and desired his neighbor seriously to consider the consequences of indulging such an unkind disposition.*
>
> *Richard took hold of his foot, and began the operation of washing it. [Baily] at first resisted; but soon became calm, and suffered Richard to wash both his feet, and wipe them with his towel. He then accompanied Richard to the door.*

Later, Baily got his shovel.

Several years later, Barnard broke his leg, and Baily cared for him during his convalescence. In 1801, when local Quakers were seeking a site for a new meetinghouse, the men each contributed two acres. The Marlborough Meetinghouse, which still stands, was built on the four-acre lot. Today, Barnard—the man who worked harder—and Baily lie near each other in its burial ground.

Now, imagine if everyone worked a little harder.

1839

FREEDOM AND THE CHURCHES

Freedom is more prized in new churches than in established ones. The Catholic Church, born under Jewish/Roman oppression, invented the Inquisition. The Puritans, seeking liberty from a corrupt state church, hanged "witches." Even Quakers, who prized freedom of conscience, attempted just a few years after their arrival in Pennsylvania to suppress critical books.

A similar transition was made by Edward Hunter (1793–1883), a Chester County farmer and early leader of the Mormon church. In 1839, Hunter defended to a hostile crowd the right of Mormon missionaries to speak. Five years later, after joining the church, he helped suppress an anti-Mormon newspaper at Nauvoo, Illinois.

"I did not care how many papers were printed in the city, if they would print the truth," wrote Hunter's church superior, Mormon prophet Joseph Smith, in his diary, "but would submit to no libels or slanders from them." Destruction of the *Nauvoo Expositor*, whose publisher charged that Smith had tried to seduce his wife, worsened relations with non-Mormon neighbors. Days later, Smith was killed by an anti-Mormon mob.

Raised near Newtown Square, Hunter was born to an unchurched family with Quaker ancestors. Edward Hunter Sr. was repelled by organized religion, his son later wrote, but believed passionately in freedom of thought. According to family history, their ancestor Robert Owen—a supporter of Oliver Cromwell—refused to swear allegiance to Charles II when the English monarchy was restored in 1660.

"[Hunter] was fond of referring to this incident in the life of his ancestor," wrote Mormon historian Orson F. Whitney. "He would relate the circumstance in his quaint, desultory way and, coming to the close, repeat the words: 'Oath of allegiance—yes, yes—refused to take it—imprisoned for five years'—and then, lifting up his hands, throwing back his head and, half shutting his eyes in a sort of dreamy ecstasy, would exclaim: 'Beautiful! Beautiful!'"

In a short autobiography, Hunter wrote that, as a boy, he had "a great dislike for going to school." His father allowed him to drop out but insisted that he learn a trade. Hunter worked at tanning hides until the tree bark tannins so irritated his skin that he was forced to quit. He studied surveying but couldn't find work. In 1816, he took a long, wandering trip through the South, where jobs were

Mormon founder Joseph Smith and his followers so impressed a Wallace farmer, Edward Hunter, that he joined Smith's church. Joining, ironically, led Hunter to reverse the belief in freedom of speech that drew him to the Mormons in the first place. *Library of Congress.*

scarce and wages low. Discouraged, he came home and managed a store in Philadelphia.

In 1817, Hunter's father was murdered. The senior Hunter, a justice of the peace, was shot by a man angered that his court testimony had cost him an inheritance. Hunter came home to manage the family farm and seems to have slipped into his father's shoes as a respected community figure. He served as a county commissioner and in the Delaware County militia. According to one biographer, he was one of two militiamen selected to escort the Marquis de Lafayette during the Frenchman's 1824 visit.

Then, perhaps feeling an urge to start over, Hunter sold the Newtown place and bought a farm in West Nantmeal. Shortly after, he came down with the near fatal case of typhoid, to which Mormon historians and Hunter descendants credit his later conversion.

"Edward's personality took on a radical change," wrote descendant William Hunter. "During his convalescence, he appeared bewildered and wandered about the plantation like a lost sheep."

He started church shopping. Hunter's neighbors were mainly Presbyterian, so he tried their churches. He investigated the Swedenborgians and the Seventh-Day Adventists. Nothing satisfied.

"I used to say they were all hewing out cisterns that would not hold water," Hunter later wrote. "The whole of [religion] has been a scene of bloodshed and murder." Hunter continued to shop, even after he met and, in 1830, married Ann Standley.

At a corner of Hunter's property facing Little Conestoga Road, a prior owner had allowed the township to build a log schoolhouse. In 1832, the building burned down when someone carelessly swept hot coals into a wooden barrel intended for ashes and left it on the porch. The township proposed rebuilding the school in stone. Hunter agreed to a ninety-nine-year lease with the sole provision that the building—which also functioned as a community center and house of worship—be open to "all persons or persuasions."

The West Nantmeal Seminary, which still stands, has been called the Wallace Seminary since 1852, when Wallace Township was created.

In 1839, the Mormons arrived. In an era of controversial new sects, they were more controversial than most. Organized in Upstate New York by Smith, who claimed that Christ had come to America after his resurrection, Mormons were aggressive proselytizers. When they learned of a chapel open to all, they sought it out.

"Immediately, the devil was raised," Hunter later wrote. "'They are a terrible people,' said the neighbors."

Not so fast, he said: "When I gave the lease for that land and helped to build that house, it was particularly agreed and stated…that people of every religion should have the privilege of meeting there. Now, those Mormons are going to have their rights, or else the lease is out and I'll take the seminary."

That would mean no school, no community center and no worship place for other congregations.

So, the Mormons spoke. And that one thing led to others. Hunter invited the missionaries to his home. That winter, Smith himself visited. And when Hunter personally drove him to the train at Downingtown, he remarked on his affection for the young missionaries.

"How is it that I am attracted to those backwoods boys?" said Hunter. "I believe I would risk my life for them." In response, Smith gave him "the most friendly look I ever got from Man."

Within a year, Hunter had been baptized. Within two years, he sold his Chester County property and moved to the new Mormon settlement at Nauvoo.

Nauvoo was not the first Mormon settlement. Mormons had previously established outposts in Ohio and Missouri, where non-Mormon residents were alarmed by the group's rapid growth. But when Mormons ordered dissidents not only out of the church but also *out of the county*, "or a more fatal calamity shall befall you," non-Mormons feared a theocracy. Other incidents followed. In 1838, the governor of Missouri declared that "the Mormons must be treated as enemies, and must be exterminated or driven from the state if necessary for the public peace."

Most of Missouri's ten thousand Mormons were forced to abandon their property and resettle at Nauvoo. That community was still getting established when Hunter arrived. With Smith's backing, Hunter was elected to the Mormon-dominated city council and became an officer in the Nauvoo Legion, a Mormon militia.

It was at Nauvoo that Smith introduced practices that came to define Mormonism among outsiders—baptism for the dead and plural marriage. Writing to a skeptical uncle, Hunter defended the practice of allowing proxy baptisms for members' deceased relatives: "I do not feel anything like denying the faith, but I hope through my service to increase it," he wrote. "Baptism for the dead is going on here every week. There was 450 baptized last week and yesterday I saw Brother Appleby from New Jersey baptized 34 times for his departed relatives."

Hunter also accepted polygamy. In 1845, he married a second wife, Laura Kauffman; in 1846, a third, Susanna Wann; and, in 1857, a fourth, Henrietta Spencer. He had children by each—fourteen in all—but no more with Ann Standley Hunter after the second marriage. Smith is variously reported as having had thirty to as many as forty-nine wives, aged fifteen to fifty-five.

Polygamy was a hard sell; some Mormons left the church over it. Brigham Young famously said that "it was the first time in my life that I had desired the grave" rather than embrace a church doctrine. (He got over it and married fifty-five women, though ten divorced him.)

Among the outraged was William Law, a former member who claimed that the Mormon prophet had made several proposals to Law's wife, Jane. According to Law, Smith had asked her "to give him half her love; she was at liberty to keep the other half for her husband." To expose the practice, Law spread this and similar stories across the first (and only) issue of the *Expositor*, published on June 7, 1844.

An emergency meeting of the city council—of which Hunter was a member—declared the paper a public nuisance and ordered it destroyed. A posse led by Nauvoo's Mormon marshal hauled the press into the street and beat it to pieces.

The council had a right to do this. At the time, the First Amendment was believed to apply only to the actions of the federal government and not to state and local authorities. Nevertheless, Mormon critics took a dimmer view.

It was Missouri all over again. Law found allies among non-Mormons. A county newspaper editorialized furiously: "Citizens arise, one and all!!! Can you stand by, and suffer such infernal devils! To rob men of their property rights, without avenging them? We have no time for comment! Everyman will make his own. Let it be with powder and ball."

Smith called out the Nauvoo Legion to defend the town but later submitted to arrest by county officials. He was in jail at nearby Carthage, charged with treason, when a mob broke in and shot him to death.

Hunter was made a bishop and, when the Mormons abandoned Illinois in 1847, personally led one hundred wagons across the plains to the Great Salt Lake. From 1851 until his death, he served as presiding bishop, the church's highest religious office. In this role, his top concern was helping church members around the world immigrate to Utah, where Mormons were free to speak and (for a time, at least) critics were absent, silent or both.

"I have acted in the priesthood and the part allotted me," said Hunter in 1853 at the laying of the cornerstone of the Salt Lake Temple, "and I hope acceptably in the sight of God and those who preside over me in this Latter-day work."

Until the end of his days, Hunter relished recounting his defense of Mormon missionaries at the Wallace Seminary. But he never renounced having helped shut down the *Expositor*.

1843

CAN THEY SUFFER?

For some Americans, few things are as horrifying as the notion that foreign ideas and laws might be relevant in a U.S. courtroom. The concept offends their sense of independence and nationhood.

But foreign ideas are hard to keep out, as demonstrated by an 1843 Chester County case in which a man was sent to prison for a year for "cruelly" beating a horse.

What is telling about the case is that, at the time, Pennsylvania had no anti-cruelty laws. The horse belonged to the man's employer so, by the book, the only possible legal charge was property damage. Despite that, Judge Thomas S. Bell (1800–1861), prosecutor Joseph Hemphill (1807–1870) and the local newspaper—all influenced by rising ideas from abroad—decried the horse's suffering and the defendant's "evil example."

"I think they found the law frustrating in that they knew what happened to the horse was wrong beyond the mere issue of destruction of property and the law did not really give them a remedy," said Dr. David Favre, editor of Animal Legal & Historical Web Center (animallaw.info) and a professor at the Michigan State University College of Law. "It took a while for the law to catch up with that emotional perspective that animal pain and suffering should count for something."

At the time, that perspective was distinctly un-American. But in the early nineteenth century, though independent for more than fifty years, the United States—especially the Northeast—still leaned toward Europe. In particular, it leaned toward Great Britain, which in 1822 was the first western nation to pass a law against animal cruelty.

In 1843, farm worker John Anderson was sentenced to a year in the Chester County Prison for a crime—animal cruelty—that didn't yet exist in Pennsylvania. Influenced by new ideas from abroad, the judge and prosecutor wanted to set an example. *Library of Congress.*

The Ill-Treatment of Cattle Act—covering horses, donkeys and most large working animals, as well as cattle—was British humanitarians' first victory in a fifty-year campaign.

Opposition to animal cruelty was part of a series of reform movements that began in the late eighteenth century. Slavery, for instance, was abolished in the British empire in 1833, capping a movement that began with the 1783 formation of that country's first abolitionist group. In 1808, after discovering that many prison inmates had committed crimes because they were mentally ill, Britain passed a County Asylums Act requiring local authorities to care for "lunatics." A century-long battle finally gave women the vote in 1918. Britain's temperance movement, however, fizzled before achieving nationwide prohibition of alcohol.

The fight against animal cruelty began in 1776 when an Anglican minister, Reverend Humphrey Primatt, published *A Dissertation on the Duty of Mercy and Sin of Cruelty to Brute Animals*, in which he argued the applicability of the Golden Rule.

"Let no views of profit, no compliance with custom and no fear of ridicule of the world, ever tempt thee to the least act of cruelty or injustice to any creature whatsoever," wrote Primatt. "But let this be your invariable rule, everywhere, and at all times, to do unto others as, in their condition, you would be done unto."

Legal protection for animals was first proposed by an English lawyer, Jeremy Bentham, in his 1789 *Introduction to the Principles of Morals and Legislation*. Bentham argued that the capacity to suffer was the primary criteria determining whether a creature deserved legal consideration.

"The question is not, 'Can they *reason?*', nor, 'Can they *talk?*', but '*Can they suffer?*" said Bentham in a piece of rhetoric still quoted by animal rights activists.

Such ideas filtered slowly through Britain's upper classes. It wasn't until 1809 that legislation was proposed, which then failed to pass Britain's House of Lords. It finally took an Irish member of parliament, Richard Martin, to push through a successful bill. Martin, who had once fought a duel to avenge the killing of a dog, was thereafter known in the United Kingdom as "Humanity Dick."

Martin subsequently collaborated in the founding of what would be the Royal Society for the Prevention of Cruelty to Animals. Intended to push enforcement of the law, the group expanded to America in 1866. But Americans had already picked up the issue.

In 1821, Maine made it a crime to "cruelly beat" any horse or cattle. According to David Favre, it was the first piece of U.S. legislation to attack cruelty without regard to ownership.

"Since common law criminal law concepts did not limit what a person did with their own property," said Favre, "this law suggested a new societal interest: concern for the animal itself." On the other hand, he noted, punishment was mild: up to $5 and/or thirty days in jail. By contrast, anyone convicted of "willfully and maliciously" maiming farm animals belonging to someone else could be fined up to $500, jailed for up to five years or both.

To Favre, the discrepancy suggests that animal cruelty had still achieved only a "bare threshold of criminality." Many people still thought that it was no big deal.

Stiffer laws followed. An 1829 New York law, for instance, demanded imprisonment of up to a year to anyone who "cruelly beat or torture(d)" his horses or cattle, though the offense was still considered a misdemeanor. Most laws covered only commercially valuable animals. In Minnesota, a person who had deliberately injured a dog escaped indictment when a judge ruled that a dog was not a "beast," as described in the law. It wasn't until 1867 that there was a law (in New York) protecting "any living creature"—livestock, pets and wild animals—against both overt cruelty and neglect, regardless of ownership.

In the meantime, concern spread as Americans discussed various proposals and considered British attempts at enforcement. From the 1830s through much of the 1850s, newspapers increasingly carried articles reporting acts of cruelty and editorials denouncing them. In August 1846, for instance, the *Philadelphia Inquirer* criticized operators of horse-drawn trolleys for overloading their vehicles in the summer heat: "The proprietors and drivers…should exercise as much humanity as possible," scolded the newspaper. "The horse is a noble and useful animal, and he should be treated accordingly."

Meanwhile, a small but persistent cohort of ministers, physicians and politicians publicly exhorted people to be kind to "brutes." Locally, Judge Bell and Joseph Hemphill would have been representative of such leaders—educated, high minded and in positions to influence events.

Born in Philadelphia, Bell moved to West Chester soon after being admitted to the bar in 1821. Any Philadelphia-trained lawyer would have been impressive in Chester County's rustic legal community, wrote local historian Douglas Harper. But Bell was also "energetic and a good speaker" and made the excellent career move of marrying Caroline Darlington, the daughter of a local judge.

Bell allied himself with the liberal branch of the Democratic-Republican Party, which controlled local politics. In 1823, he was appointed district attorney for Chester County. In 1837, Bell represented Chester and Montgomery Counties at a convention to revise the state constitution. The following year, he was a Democratic leader during the so-called Buckshot War, in which the Anti-Masonic Party attempted to seize control of the legislature despite having lost the election. (Called out to restore order, eight hundred members of the state militia arrived at Harrisburg carrying muskets loaded with buckshot.) In 1848, an anonymous poet, writing in the *American Republican* newspaper, used Bell's role in the incident to propose him as a candidate for governor: "Take T.S. Bell, he'll do it well / He's talented and true, sirs / With him to steer the ship of state / we're rescued from disgrace, sirs."

Appointed president judge for Chester and Delaware Counties in 1839, Bell served until 1846 and then resigned to serve five years on the state supreme court. One example of his thinking came in an 1842 case in which the owners of several local cotton mills had several employees indicted for "conspiracy" to raise their wages by forming a union. Bell instructed the jury that there was no law forbidding this: "Peaceably to meet and discuss the proper steps to be adopted for the protection or advancement of their common interests can never be objected against American citizens as an offense."

Born in West Chester, Joseph Hemphill came from a family of lawyers. In 1848, he ran unsuccessfully for Congress as a Locofoco, a liberal splinter group of the Democratic Party that had a pro-reform and pro-labor platform. Like Bell, Hemphill was an active abolitionist. In the 1840s, he signed a petition to the legislature from the Chester County Bar favoring abolition of the death penalty.

"His mind was of an eminently judicial cast," wrote the *Daily Local News* at Hemphill's death, "and had he reached the bench, we have reason to believe he would have proven a worthy successor to the distinguished citizens of Chester County."

Bell and Hemphill were also brothers-in-law. In 1830, Bell had married Hemphill's sister, Keziah, as his second wife.

Both men were likely to have been familiar with and sympathetic to the emerging concept of animal rights. In any case, they did not let it pass when, in August 1843, local farmer Enos Smedley complained that a hired hand, John Anderson, had abused his horse.

Testimony has been lost, but a newspaper account of *Commonwealth v. John Anderson* reported that the man had been harrowing a cornfield, a laborious task that involved dragging a spiked board across the ground to remove roots and smooth it for planting. The horse was described as "a tractable and good worker," though perhaps not on that particular day. Anderson, the jury ruled, "unlawfully, willfully, maliciously, cruelly and publicly did beat, wound and ill-treat and one of the eyes of the said horse then and there did destroy and put out, to the great damage of the said Enos Smedley, to the evil example of all others in like cases offending and against the peace and dignity of the Commonwealth of Pennsylvania." (Probably the jury merely voted "guilty" to a charge whose phrasing was that of the judge and prosecutor.)

The *Daily Local News* chimed in, too. "We hope that the example will not be disregarded," wrote an editor, "as cases daily occur in which unfeeling persons render themselves liable to punishment for wanton cruelty to dumb animals."

Which, again, was saying a lot—considering that the law as written could punish Anderson only for property damage. But new ideas were afoot.

1843

Defending Monogamy

Monogamy, scientists tell us, is not the natural condition of human beings. But its spirited public defense is quite natural to politicians and other community leaders, who rarely suffer backlash for protecting what few supposedly like.

A local example is the Battle Axes, a nineteenth-century religious sect whose members embraced—loudly, publicly and *in the nude*—polygamy and communism. (Of the two, polygamy upset people most.) An 1843 crackdown pleased local ministers immensely and did no harm to the careers of county officials.

In addition, the episode left a tangible legacy: architect Thomas U. Walter's 1846 Chester County Courthouse, still in use today.

Battle Axe-ism was the creation of Theophilus R. Gates, a New England minister who had preached at Baptist churches in Virginia. In the late 1830s, however, Gates proclaimed his own new religion. Its central tenet was the sinfulness of marriage, which Gates identified as a relic of the fall from Eden.

According to Gates, the atoning death and resurrection of Christ meant that humanity had been forgiven for the Original Sin of apple eating and, therefore, could now live in perfect sinlessness. Marriage, however, presented an obstacle to perfection by focusing love on individuals.

"Falling in love, now so common in the world, is in every case an enchantment of the devil, the direct tendency of which is to love and regard a creature more than the Creator," wrote Gates.

Above: Chester County's 1846 courthouse is the most tangible legacy of the Battle Axes, a cult that openly practiced polygamy and communism. Also alive and well is the impulse of community leaders to pontificate about such behavior. *Library of Congress.*

Right: The apostle of "free love," Theophilus R. Gates was a former Baptist who thought marriage obsolete because it focused love on human beings that should belong to God. In its place, he favored frequent swapping of sexual partners. *Mark E. Dixon.*

To protect the primacy of God, Gates favored a more generalized affection for human beings. It would be better, he insisted, to change partners twenty times than remain with an incompatible mate "in the order of the devil, and in his dominions on the road to hell."

Gates called this "complex" marriage. (But then, what marriage isn't?)

Perfectionism wasn't a new concept. In the seventeenth century, some of the first Quakers had voiced similar ideas, going naked in the streets to demonstrate their restoration to Eden-like innocence. But Quakers never abandoned marriage. Moreover, they disciplined fornication and adultery with a zeal that contributed to their decline.

The early nineteenth century, however, was a time of new ideas and new adaptations of old ideas. Among the sixty to seventy utopian movements at the time was Millerism, whose proponent (William Miller) predicted the return of Jesus sometime in 1843 or 1844; transcendentalism, which claimed an ideal spiritual reality knowable only through intuition; and Shakerism, which promised salvation through celibacy, work and dance. Most radical of all, perhaps, were abolitionism, temperance and women's rights.

Gates was briefly allied with John Humphrey Noyes, who founded the Oneida community in Upstate New York. While mostly agreeing about marriage and private property, Gates and Noyes ultimately split over how best to deal with the byproducts of polygamy.

Noyes favored raising children communally to regard all adults as their mothers and fathers. (His Oneida community eventually became a joint-stock company and survives today as a manufacturer of silverware.) Gates favored birth control by the withdrawal method. His idea was that young women would pair off with older men who had mastered ejaculatory control and, thus, could avoid impregnating them. Unskilled younger men would practice with older, presumably infertile women.

In short, it was a perfect sort of faith for middle-aged men in unhappy marriages. Gates, whose wife doubted his sanity, began this strange ministry when he was about fifty.

In June 1837, Gates started a small newspaper, the *Battle Axe and Weapons of War*, in which he declared that the bond of husband and wife was a mere fashion that "passeth away." (The title was drawn from the book of Jeremiah: "Thou art my battle-axe and weapon of war.") Gates peddled his paper on the streets of Philadelphia for five cents per copy though with limited success—until he met young, pretty Hannah Williamson.

Williamson, a daughter of an old Quaker family near Dilworthtown, had left her parents to live independently in Philadelphia. An unmarried woman living alone was often regarded as a prostitute, and Williamson has been described as one. Whatever the truth, she became Gates's zealous convert.

Philadelphia, though, seems to have been a hard nut to crack. After publishing three issues of the *Battle Axe*, Gates and Williamson left the city and set up camp near Valley Forge, on the present site of the Glenhardie Country Club. Here and in North Coventry Township, they made a few dozen converts among local farmers.

One convert was William Stubblebine, who was identified by Magdelene Snyder, another believer, as her "soul mate." Snyder then moved into Stubblebine's house. The pair evidently expected to share house and table amicably with Stubblebine's wife, Catherine, and their six children. But Mrs. Stubblebine found this unacceptable and moved to her brother's, taking the children.

Another near convert was Aaron Morton, a respected landowner, father of ten and the grandson of a signer of the Declaration of Independence. Morton, who lived in Ridley Township, embraced Gates's ideas. But when pressed to choose between fidelity to his wife and a life that would include Williamson—and perhaps others—Morton slit his own throat. When word of this got around, Gates and Williamson fled the township, reportedly with local residents hissing their carriage as it passed.

As time passed—and as Gates got older—his passion declined. He became content to live in relative quiet among the Battle Axes, who met mostly around the village of Shenkel in North Coventry. Leadership passed to Williamson, who lived with two brothers in a small cabin in a part of the township still known as "Free Love Valley." Williamson led the group with a fanaticism that even Gates was never able to match.

It was Williamson who stood up in the Shenkel Church one Sunday and, in the middle of the pastor's sermon, laid a pile of Battle Axe pamphlets on the pulpit before him. When the minister snorted, "Away with that abominable stuff" and swept the papers onto the floor, Williamson admonished him, "I warn you not to sin the message of God away."

Another time, after the Shenkel pastor had continued to condemn the Battle Axes, Williamson and a group of followers walked naked up the aisle in declaration of their beliefs.

Apparently, Williamson also devised the group's only ritual. This was usually conducted at her cabin, where each member disrobed and then marched in single file—looking neither right nor left—to a small pond, whose waters represented purity. There, immersed in purity, their affections to one another were unrestricted—so unrestricted, in fact, that William

Rhoads, a sheriff in neighboring Berks County, once invaded the ceremony with a bullwhip.

Eventually, the neighbors had enough. Samuel Willauer, the local justice of the peace, gathered enough evidence to charge four Battle Axes with adultery and/or fornication—both offenses "against the peace and dignity of the Commonwealth."

David Stubblebine, a married brother of William, was accused of adultery with Hannah Williamson and her sister, Lydia. Lydia was also charged with fornication. Another Stubblebine brother, Jacob, and Samuel Barde were charged with fornication with the Williamsons. Jacob Stubblebine was also charged with having had relations with Elizabeth Stubblebine, his sister.

In a time before lap dancing and Internet porn, this sort of entertainment was as good as it got. When the cases came to trial in February 1843, the tiny 1785 courthouse on High Street in West Chester was jammed. Proposals to enlarge or replace the structure had been heard throughout the 1830s to no end. Now, though, the *Village Record* newspaper reported that the building "was much too small to afford seats to the spectators—and more than one old taxpayer, after standing until his legs ached, was heard to say something about better accommodations and the propriety of having a more commodious courthouse."

Alas, the trial was over soon after it began. David Stubblebine, Barde and Williamson admitted the charges and were quickly convicted, relieving prosecutor Joseph Hemphill of any need to go into juicy details. Jacob Stubblebine was acquitted. Thomas Bell, the president judge, and his two associate judges, Jesse Sharp and Thomas Jones, sentenced the three to prison sentences that ranged from five to eighteen months.

Afterward, all returned to Free Love Valley, but the steam seems to have gone out of the movement. Gates died in 1846. And Hannah Williamson, after being roughly ejected from a Methodist camp meeting at Shafer's Grove in 1854, moved west seeking new converts.

For local officials, there was apparently no price for invading the Battle Axes' privacy. Three years after the trial, Bell was named to the Pennsylvania Supreme Court. Sharp and Jones continued on until their timely retirements. Hemphill lost his 1846 race for Congress—not, said the *American Republican* newspaper, because of his character or conduct but because he ran on the Locofoco ticket in a Whig district. Willauer continued as a justice and, when he died in 1870, was remembered for "an active and useful life."

The cornerstone of the new courthouse was laid in 1846. Monogamy, beleaguered though it may be, lives on.

1847

QUALITY CAME SECOND

Business and ethics make for an awkward mix. One is about creating and satisfying trivial wants; the other, about putting them aside.

This conundrum has deep roots in the Delaware Valley. Three hundred years ago, early opponents of slavery chose to wear hemp rather than better fabrics made by slaves. This movement reached its height in the 1850s when George W. Taylor (1803–1891) set up a cotton mill in Chester County to supply his "free labor" store in Philadelphia. With adequate supplies of merchandise, Taylor and his supporters believed, ethical shopping could strangle slavery without firing a shot.

The business was a headache. Raw materials were hard to obtain. Delivery was undependable. And even conscientious Quaker women were critical of defective weaving, ugly patterns and colors that faded. Abolitionist Lucretia Mott—whose husband, James, got out of the cotton trade to protest slavery—was blunt. "Free sugar," she wrote, "was not always as free from other taints as from that of slavery; and free calicoes could seldom be called handsome, even by the most enthusiastic; free umbrellas were hideous to look upon, and free candies, an abomination."

Taylor learned retailing and antislavery as a boy. Born to a farm family in Radnor, he moved in 1812 to Kaolin in southern Chester County, where his father, Jacob, ran a store. The Taylors did not belong to any church until George was twelve, when he and his mother were accepted at New Garden Friends Meeting. Jacob Taylor attended but never joined.

Young George liked money. As a child, he resisted smallpox vaccination, which involved cutting his arm. His father promised him three silver dollars

Abolitionist William Lloyd Garrison dismissed as a "waste of time and talent" Chester County native George Taylor's effort to win shoppers to merchandise untainted by slavery. Taylor eventually came to agree with him. *Library of Congress.*

Abolitionist Lucretia Mott was fully in sympathy with the free labor concept, but she was also a careful shopper. Offered candy that was free of any taint of slave-grown sugar, she tasted the stuff and pronounced it "an abomination." *Library of Congress.*

if he cooperated. Eventually, he saved enough to buy several ewes, whose wool and lambs he sold to buy a watch and a dictionary. But it wasn't just the money. Carrying grain to the mill one day, Taylor stopped at the home of a free black family, where he found the owner ill and his wife and children nearly destitute. He gave the man all of the money he had—"some three or four dollars"—and later went back with more.

"I learned afterward that it was sufficient for their needs until he recovered," Taylor wrote in his autobiography. When he learned years later that one of the boys had grown up to be a Methodist minister, Taylor decided that Providence had been at work.

After Taylor joined the Quakers, he began using the plain language—"thee" and "thou," rather than "you," when speaking to an individual. Most Quakers had dropped "thou," the nominative form, though doing so was grammatically incorrect. Taylor's sisters laughed at him, but he considered it a religious duty to speak properly and thou'd for the rest of his life.

Taylor made up his mind early about slavery. Embracing the argument of John Woolman (1720–1772) that using slave products made one as guilty as the slave owner, he used flax goods instead of cotton and abstained from sugar, rice and coffee.

Finished at the common school, Taylor taught in the neighborhood. But as he did so, he spent part of his income for mathematics instruction from Enoch Lewis (1776–1858) of New Garden, a respected teacher and a dedicated antislavery man. In 1803, when his annual salary was $500, Lewis paid $400 for the freedom of a runaway slave. His wife, Alice, was known when shopping to "discriminate…between the produce of free or slave labor."

Lewis believed in the interconnectedness of all things. So it was not thought odd when he brought a former slave to meet with his mathematics students and describe his experiences. It seems likely that Lewis's mathematics instruction—which included economics—would have included the thinking then current among Quakers that slavery wasn't merely evil but also financially inefficient.

After eight months with Lewis, Taylor "completed a full and thorough course in mathematics and was qualified to teach all its branches." He taught for seven years in Quaker schools and then, in 1834, began publishing religious tracts and a Quaker newspaper. He also became involved in what would be his life's mission.

Before 1827, the free-labor idea had been the notion of a few very observant Quakers. Benjamin Lay (circa 1681–1759) had refused to eat food produced by slave labor and, just as peculiar, lived in a cave. Henry Drinker (1757–1822) lost a fortune in the 1790s trying to develop maple sugar as a viable substitute for slave-grown sugar. In London Grove, two Quaker families planted their own cotton, producing a small bale that, when processed, yielded enough for four or five shirts. (The plants died in the fall.)

The Philadelphia Free Produce Association intended to take the effort up a notch. Rather than operating a store, however, the group batched believers' orders and then found manufacturers to fill them. Often, they had to pay upfront and hope not to be too surprised by what arrived. Shipments were stored at members' homes until they were picked up. In 1847, Taylor saw an opportunity to live out his beliefs. He opened a free-labor store, thereby becoming the movement's public face.

"From the very outset, manufacturing presented difficulties," wrote movement historian Ruth Nuermberger. Most cotton manufacturers weren't eager to run this unknown "free" product through their machinery. (Would it, for instance, be equally free of seeds and other plant trash?) Fewer were willing to clear machines of slave cotton before running through a few bales of free. Taylor's solution was to throw away fabric from the beginning and the end of each run rather than offer mixed fabric.

British manufacturing was costly. Even if cotton was grown in the United States, customs charged a 30 percent duty on fabric, plus the cost of shipping.

"Terminology in the two countries differed," wrote Nuermberger, "so that when Taylor would ask for a particular cloth by name, [his supplier] would send something entirely different."

Plus, Taylor was selling primarily to Quakers, who would dress only in their distinctive colors: brown, gray and drab. Many suppliers didn't understand this quirk in the Philadelphia market and sent the usual array of blue, red, green, yellow and purple fabrics, for which Taylor found no buyers. Yet customers also demanded quality.

"The printed linen cambrics," Taylor wrote his British supplier in 1852, "appear to be very badly printed…so much so that ladies who wanted dresses of them would not take them."

Taylor and his supporters traveled extensively, seeking out suppliers and offering above-market prices. In 1850, after traveling to the West Indies seeking free sugar, molasses and cotton, he reported back that the planters of St. Croix—a Danish possession that had abolished slavery two years earlier—were "intelligent, energetic and liberal minded…and their sugar and molasses are of the very best quality." Unfortunately, being ignorant of sugar growing, he'd come two months before the harvest and so couldn't bring back samples. (Oops.) Puerto Rico, meanwhile, belonged to Spain, which permitted slavery; no planters there, he learned, raised free cotton. Supply was always a problem.

Meanwhile, Taylor had started a monthly newspaper, the *Non-Slaveholder*, to promote the movement and tell readers where to buy free goods. In 1845, the paper ran a long report from Cairo explaining that, while slaves existed in Egypt, the country's cotton should be considered free. Egyptian slaves, wrote William Jay, were usually household servants, while agricultural workers were mostly Arabs (and free).

This was way more than retail. Taylor and his supporters were trying to jump-start a *movement*. If they could move just part of the U.S. market off slave products, the idea could catch on in Britain, which bought half of America's cotton. Slavery, they remembered, had been abolished in the British empire after English housewives had boycotted sugar.

Believing that he needed full control over manufacturing, Taylor in 1854 raised $9,000 from investors, added $3,000 of his own and leased Henry Webster's mill north of Unionville. But in its first full year, the mill spun just seventy bales. Then, in 1857, a financial panic closed the banks. Taylor paid workers with cloth, which they bartered for groceries. The mill was opened again in 1859 but was closed for good when the Civil War cut off supplies and, ultimately, its rationale. The machinery was sold in 1862, with all investors taking a loss. Taylor continued the store until 1867 and then retired to farm.

Free labor's fatal blow came from within the antislavery movement. In 1850, William Lloyd Garrison—who had endorsed the concept in the 1830s—dismissed it as a "waste of time and talent" and proponents as moralistic fussbudgets who turned off potential abolitionist converts. By then, the combative Garrison had shifted the antislavery movement from Quakers' traditional inward focus ("changing yourself") to fugitive slave legislation and the admission of new states ("changing them"). Self-denial didn't offer the same thrill.

Late in life, reading a forty-year-old letter from an enthusiastic free-labor ally, a far more experienced Taylor commented, "I am led to admire his expanded philanthropy, but at the same time my experience in the 20 years effort in the Free Labor cause has shown me how hard it [was] to rally even the best of people."

Business and ethics, he had learned, just didn't mix well.

1852

GETTING RID OF NATHAN

Today, everyone loves the abolitionists, but we don't have to live with them. To those who endured their company, abolitionists were just as annoying as any loud modern activist promoting a cause.

Locally, abolitionist Nathan Evans (1782–1852) of Willistown was a headache to fellow Quakers for at least twenty years. In 1846, tired of listening to him drone on about slavery every Sunday, they disowned him. Forced by church superiors to take him back, Willistown disowned Evans again in 1852.

And this, mind you, occurred in an antislavery church. The Willistown Quakers agreed with his message if not his obsession with the subject. Quakers had forbidden members to own slaves in the 1770s and had provided pivotal support for Pennsylvania's 1780 abolition law. In 1851, Philadelphia-area Quakers advised members to ignore the Fugitive Slave Law, which required Northerners to help slave owners recover their property: "We decline…to be made the instruments of a law which requires…returning a human being into a bondage which we believe is not sanctioned by divine authority."

But even Quakers found Nathan Evans hard to take.

Born in New Jersey, Evans moved to Lower Merion as a child. Not long after his 1831 marriage to Zillah Maule, the couple moved to a farm at Providence and Marlborough Roads in Willistown.

When and why Evans became an abolitionist was not recorded. But he was sympathetic to the cause's radical fringe as early as 1832, when he wrote an approving letter to William Lloyd Garrison's new newspaper, the *Liberator*.

Founded in 1831, the *Liberator* was controversial for the severe language with which Garrison addressed slaveholders. Officially, Garrison opposed

In the 1840s, Willistown Quakers—who now rest in their burial ground, forever free of Nathan Evans's rants—were so tired of listening to the rabid abolitionist that a frustrated few carried him from the meetinghouse. *Mark E. Dixon.*

violence. But that opposition was easy to miss when he made statements such as this: "Our slaves have the best reason to assert their rights by violent measures, inasmuch as they are more oppressed than others." When Virginia slave Nat Turner led a rebellion that killed fifty-five whites, southerners blamed Garrison's newspaper. Thereafter, free blacks in the South were forbidden to receive the *Liberator*, and several southern governors and senators tried to suppress it entirely.

But Evans was a fan. "I hope thou mayest be favored from on high…in one of the best of causes to undo the heavy burdens and let the oppressed go free," Evans wrote Garrison. "I wish there was a *Liberator* in every dwelling in Pennsylvania."

Garrison's newspaper, Evans hoped, might be a cure for what he perceived as his neighbors' racism and consequent reluctance to press vigorously for abolition.

"The idea that [African Americans] are not fit to be free, prevails to a most astonishing extent," wrote the Willistown farmer, "although our state has tried the experiment and found no inconvenience, as well as [New England], but on the contrary, a blessing has followed that ought to flash conviction in the mind of all those whose minds are not darkened by prejudice."

By then, Evans's home was already a stop on the Underground Railroad. The route ran to his door from Bartholomew Fussell, a Kennett Square physician, who received runaways from the notorious Thomas Garrett at Wilmington. From Willistown, separate lines ran north to Phoenixville and east to the offices of the Pennsylvania Anti-Slavery Society in Philadelphia.

Evans aided the escape of 150 fugitives, according to Underground Railroad historian Robert Smedley, and was active in this work before 1839. In that year, wrote Smedley, Evans, "who had for years made frequent trips to Philadelphia with large numbers of fugitives," solicited James Lewis of Marple to make Lewis's home an intermediate stop.

Lewis agreed and, soon after, made an initial run with Evans in a wagon carrying eight runaways. On the way, Evans shared his experience, introducing Lewis to other participants and showing him how to recognize threats, such as the inquisitive-looking man who watched them at one stop. (They moved on and later learned that the first stop had been raided.) Obviously, Evans was a veteran.

At Willistown Meeting, Evans was a problem for two reasons.

As a group, Quakers remained committed to the vision of John Woolman (1720–1772), a religious mystic from New Jersey who had been a catalyst in the Quakers' emancipation of their own slaves.

Driven by religious visions, Woolman made his first stand against slavery in the early 1740s when he declined another Quaker's request to write a bill of sale for a slave. "I spoke to him in goodwill," wrote Woolman in his journal, "and he told me that keeping slaves was not altogether agreeable to his mind; but that the slave being a gift made to his wife he had accepted her." From this and similar encounters, Woolman concluded that even slave owners harbored doubts, which presented an opportunity if they were approached in a friendly way. In 1758, Woolman was appointed to a committee "to visit all Friends who hold slaves and persuade them to set their slaves at liberty." Eventually, after years of work, this committee was successful.

The Quaker precedent encouraged Pennsylvania legislators to ease slavery out the door. To reduce opposition, slave owners were allowed to keep existing slaves, as well as those slaves' children, until the latter reached twenty-eight. It doesn't sound particularly progressive, but in fact, slavery declined rapidly and was virtually extinct in the state by 1810.

Believing slavery could be abolished nonviolently did not seem naive in the enthusiasm of the Revolutionary era. Southern Founding Fathers such as Jefferson, Madison and Washington supported emancipation, and as late as 1827, there were 140 antislavery societies in the South. Great Britain had abolished slavery by legislation in 1834. But southern willingness to consider emancipation withered with the Turner revolt and with the increasingly harsh tone of abolitionists.

That was the second problem: Evans's mouth. Quaker meetings operate by consensus. In such an environment, soft words and a presumption of other members' good intentions are more effective than accusations.

But that wasn't Evans's style. He liked to talk, and he had one subject. If the meetinghouse roof needed repair, Nathan might observe that the slaves had no proper roofs over their heads, either. If a couple applied to be married, Nathan could interject that slaves had no such right. Some Willistown Quakers may even have hesitated to say good morning to Nathan for fear they'd get a speech: "A 'good morning,' thee says? Well, of course it's a good morning to thee. Thee is free and is not wearing chains on thy hands and on thy feet. But does thee think it is a 'good morning' for the slaves?" Yadda, yadda, yadda.

Even Smedley admitted that, while "earnest, sincere and truthful," Evans could also be "tedious."

Evans probably wanted to see some action from the supposedly antislavery Willistown Quakers. Some risk taking. Some…well…lawbreaking. Their scrupulousness about obeying the law likely seemed too convenient. He may have been right. Those caught helping runaways could lose their property. (Garrett, caught and convicted in 1848, lost virtually everything.) And the prosperous Willistown farmers—with big stone houses, big farms and big families—had a lot to lose.

By 1845, Willistown had had enough of Evans. The congregation charged him with "disorderly conduct in meeting" and disowned him. The specific charges, which were not recorded, were insufficient in the opinion of the Concord Quarterly Meeting, which acted as an appeals court. Concord ruled that Evans's disownment "ought not to be sustained." Translation: Willistown had to take him back.

Moreover, Willistown had to keep listening. On one occasion, wrote Smedley, when Evans was detailing the plight of a recent group of refugees—"poorly clad, tired and hungry, their flesh bearing the marks of the lash…a mother, whose child had been torn from her and sold to traders"—and criticizing Willistown's supposed indifference, one elder sighed, "Have a little mercy on us."

Perhaps it was then, when Willistown really felt stuck with Nathan Evans, that something quite unQuakerly happened at the old meetinghouse on Goshen Road. When Evans rose (again!) to speak one Sunday, two exasperated men seized him and carried him outside. As he went, Evans was heard to say, "My Master rode on one jackass and now I ride on two!"

On another occasion, Evans is alleged to have wondered aloud whether the "W.M." engraved on the meetinghouse's 1798 date stone stood for "Willistown Meeting" or for "Wicked Men."

In August 1851, the meeting accused Evans of "disturbing Religious Meetings by delivering long, tedious, unprofitable discourses." He might have survived that charge, but Evans had also been observed "reading a newspaper in the publick meeting"—properly, a time for prayer—and refusing to put the paper away. Worse, he did this at a quarterly meeting, which had saved him in 1846 but would now be less sympathetic. Compounding things, Evans refused to leave the room, as required, so members could discuss his case.

In September, he again refused to leave the room. In October, when Evans still refused to budge, the meeting appointed a committee—presumably in his presence—to deal with him. He was formally disowned in January 1852.

Emotions ran high everywhere. The Fugitive Slave Law had been passed in 1850. Harriet Beecher Stowe's *Uncle Tom's Cabin* had been published in May. In September, when Evans was refusing to move from his bench, a slave owner was killed at Christiana, Lancaster County, while retrieving runaways. In October, abolitionists had stormed a jail in Syracuse, New York, to free a fugitive.

Perhaps Evans had issues with authority. Several historians have observed that abolitionism attracted people with personal problems. Historian Peter Walker looked at abolitionists Jane Swisshelm, Moncure Conway and Henry Wright and found sexual repression (Swisshelm), domineering fathers (Conway) and delusions of personal perfection (Wright). Even Frederick Douglass, wrote Walker, had personal motivations, using abolition to drive himself "as far toward the center of white American society as the fact of his being black permitted."

It was Douglass's paper, the *North Star*, that in October 1851 published a long, rambling letter in which Nathan Evans defended the Christiana rioters against worshippers of "the Moloch of slavery, on whose bloody altar the American republic has made more offerings than any other nation of modern times."

In July 1852, Evans again told the Quakers that he would appeal, but he died in September while the appeal was pending. To this final verdict, the Quakers of Willistown may have silently replied, "Amen."

1854

MOVING ISAAC

Americans love celebrities. And if the celebrities are dead…well, that hardly matters.

If it were otherwise, nobody would visit Ben Franklin's grave, tour Graceland or gawk at the former mansions of dead Hollywood stars. Locally, civic leaders in 1850s West Chester made use of this fascination: they recruited a local dead celebrity—Major Isaac D. Barnard (1791–1834), a hero of the War of 1812—to popularize Oaklands, a new cemetery on the borough's northern outskirts. Barnard's bones were removed from an unmarked grave at a Quaker burial ground and reburied with great fanfare at Oaklands. Sales took off.

"Since Barnard had left no immediate family to object to the removal, it was a done deal," wrote West Chester historian Douglas R. Harper.

The event was a signal. For dead West Cestrians, Oaklands was the place to be. After the relocation of Barnard's bones, many families disinterred their dead from the town's old burial grounds and reburied them in family lots at Oaklands. The former burial grounds are now covered with houses.

Born in Delaware County, Barnard spent his youth on a farm near Chester, where his father served as sheriff at the county seat. In 1800, James Barnard was appointed clerk of the county court, and the family moved into the borough. Young Isaac quit school at thirteen to clerk in his father's office. After his father's death, Barnard continued clerking until 1811, when he began to study law.

In March 1812, Barnard received a captain's commission in the Fourteenth U.S. Infantry. Anticipating war with Great Britain, the federal government

The War of 1812 hero Major Isaac Barnard was posthumously useful for Oaklands Cemetery in 1854. Founders of the new and struggling cemetery moved Barnard from another burial ground and erected this marble obelisk over his bones. Barnard's celebrity caused business to pick up nicely. *Mark E. Dixon.*

was increasing the size of its army. Barnard's first assignment was to go to West Chester and enlist seventy men.

The War of 1812 was not popular in the Northeast. War meant a virtual shutdown of international trade, which hurt bankers, manufacturers and ship owners, of which the Philadelphia area had more than its share. So, Barnard's placement of ads in the *Chester & Delaware Federalist* newspaper headlined "Soldiers? Soldiers?" got some notice and, apparently, not all in a good way.

"The war was entered into by the persons in power…more for the sake of supporting the tottering and declining popularity of [their party] than from patriotic views," wrote the editor. Nevertheless, he refrained from blaming Barnard who, he conceded, had not used deceitful recruiting tactics and did not flog those he signed.

Barnard got his seventy.

In 1813, Barnard was present at the Battle of Fort George, in which U.S. troops captured a British fort on the western shore of Lake Ontario. Things did not go as well at the subsequent Battle of Beaver Dams, during which a portion of Barnard's regiment and most of its officers were captured. That left Barnard in command of what remained of the unit, promoted to major. In the highlight of his military career, at the Battle of Lyon's Creek near Niagara Falls, Barnard led 900 Americans in a frontal assault against 1,200 British grenadiers, who fled.

"All did their duty," reported Barnard's commanding officer, "but the handsome manner in which Major Barnard brought his regiment into action…deserve[s] particular notice."

After the war, Barnard declined a permanent position with a downsized army. Admitted to the bar in 1815, he soon found—as veterans often do—that other veterans were prepared to help pave the way for their own. Colonel Cromwell Pearce, elected Chester County sheriff in 1816, saw to it that Barnard was appointed deputy district attorney. In 1820, Barnard was elected to the state senate.

On the side, Barnard was colonel of the Chester County militia; led the effort to erect a monument that still stands at the site of the Paoli Massacre; participated in ceremonies welcoming the Marquis de Lafayette in 1824; was a director of the Bank of Chester County; and served on a committee to commemorate the landing of William Penn. All of this can be taken as proof that Barnard was well liked.

He rose quickly. In 1826, Barnard was appointed to the governor's cabinet. The next year, the legislature appointed him to the U.S. Senate, where he was a supporter of Andrew Jackson, another veteran of the War of 1812. In Pennsylvania, there was talk of Barnard running for governor. But his health began to fail. He resigned from the Senate in 1831 and died in West Chester three years later. His obituary in the *American Republican* newspaper lamented his "uprightness and purity of purpose," his bravery, his honesty and his patriotism but did not specify a cause of death. Barnard, whose ancestors had been Quaker even though he was not, was buried at the Friends burying ground on North High Street.

And there he lay for twenty years. Meanwhile, West Chester was growing, and its burial grounds—most of them in the southwest corner of the village—were filling.

The "rural cemetery" movement reached West Chester later than in the big cities. It had begun in 1831, when Boston opened Mount Auburn Cemetery, whose founders believed that quiet, landscaped rural locations were better suited to commemorating the dead than tightly packed urban graveyards. Perhaps this was pure Victorian sentimentality. Or perhaps it was a convenient rationale for urban leaders with other plans for scarce land. In any case, the trend spread. Philadelphia opened Laurel Hill Cemetery in 1836. Fifteen years later, West Chester was ready. In January 1851, several leading citizens called a public meeting at Cabinet Hall to discuss burial grounds.

Cabinet Hall was the home of the Chester County Cabinet of Natural Sciences, a local version of the Franklin Institute. Both were clubs for educated gentlemen interested in scientific progress and civic improvements. The cabinet was founded by an Enlightenment-oriented physician, William Darlington, and several other physicians were members. Likely they were the source of a report to the British government warning about the health hazards of burial grounds—one that a cabinet member shared with the gathering.

"The deleterious gas or miasma escaping continually from all graveyards affords another reason why it is incumbent on us to provide a more remote as well as retired spot for a depository of the dead," the report noted. That, plus a lengthy recitation of ancient burial practices—the habit of the ancient Jews of setting aside gardens for royal tombs, for instance—and a review of the new cemeteries opening elsewhere was enough for West Chester's thinking people.

In April, Oaklands was incorporated as a nonprofit and purchased twenty-three acres of land about 1.5 miles from the center of the borough. The burgesses then moved quickly, announcing in July that an 1844 ordinance prohibiting burials in the center of town—Matlack to New Street and Barnard to Chestnut Street—would be "rigidly enforced." The ordinance did not require bodies already buried to be exhumed.

This wasn't universally popular. Catholic Christ Church was within the proscribed boundaries, and not long after the burgesses acted, one of its families secretly buried their mother next to the remains of their previously deceased father. A constable caught them in the act, and those responsible were fined. (Still, the illegally buried woman stayed where she was.) Some Catholics thought that the Protestants had gotten special consideration; the Episcopalian, Methodist, Baptist and Quaker burial grounds were all outside of the forbidden zone.

Oaklands tried to ease the transition by offering sections set aside for the exclusive use of the various churches. But there was continued grumbling that those involved were out for profit. "It seems that West Chester cannot even bury its dead with unanimity," lamented the *American Republican* newspaper.

Even as Oaklands was dedicated in December 1853, burials seem to have continued in the old places. There was even a hint of desperation from the managers, who pleaded at the dedication, "We hope that the different religious congregations will take means to prevent burials in their graveyards, and that every family having ability will at once become interested in our new cemetery." Meanwhile, Oaklands was in the red.

The cabinet members probably decided that this thing needed a little help.

In July 1854, Darlington chaired another public meeting to propose that Barnard's remains be moved to Oaklands, which, according to the *Village Record* newspaper, had "liberally donated a suitable lot for the purpose." It would set a good example for the young, claimed the organizers, who authorized a committee to begin fundraising for a monument on Barnard's new grave.

There was precedent for this sort of publicity stunt. In 1838, the remains of Charles Thomson, secretary of the Continental Congress, were moved to Laurel Hill Cemetery from the Harriton House burial ground in Bryn Mawr. (Doubt remains, however, about whether workers got the right bones from Harriton's unmarked graveyard.)

The date was set for October 19, the fortieth anniversary of the Battle of Lyon's Creek. In anticipation, Barnard's remains were dug up and placed in a new walnut coffin. At least, that was the story. In 1906, Captain Benjamin H. Sweney, a Civil War veteran, told the *Daily Local News* that he had been present at the exhumation and went home with souvenirs—"a fine lock of the General's hair [which soon crumbled to dust] and a brass hinge off the old coffin." Factor in other souvenir hunters and who knows what went where.

But the ceremony was fine: a military procession, followed by the hearse, clergy, relatives, the organizing committee, surviving War of 1812 veterans and the citizenry. All marched to Oaklands, where Barnard was laid beneath a new marble obelisk, while Darlington extolled his deeds and the "beautiful rural repository of the dead" where he was now laid.

With enforcement of the ordinances and families anxious to keep their deceased relatives together, business picked up nicely. When Oaklands' managers assembled for their next annual meeting, they found that there had been fifty-two burials, including thirty-six transfers from other graveyards. The power of celebrity at work.

1858

Party Politics

Starting a new political party isn't rocket science. Just take one political party that's gotten too big, been in power too long and cut too many corners. Then organize its malcontents.

In 1858, one such malcontent was John Hickman (1810–1875), a U.S. congressman from West Chester. Hickman started out his political career as a Democrat. But his split with pro-southern party leaders was the wedge that inspired local Know-Nothings, Whigs and disaffected Democrats to coalesce into the new Republican Party of Chester County—which, of course, has mostly controlled county government ever since.

Local Democrats were hardly sorry to see him go, although they might have fared better had he stayed.

"Hickman has proved himself only 'a kind of Democrat,' and that of the poorest and shakiest kind," wrote John Hodgson, editor of the *Jeffersonian*, a Democratic newspaper, "a kind that approximates so nearly to a Black Republican that it is scarcely possible to distinguish one from the other."

As a Republican, Hickman exhibited the fervency of the converted. In the early days of the Civil War, he criticized the Lincoln administration's slowness to move against the Confederacy. After emancipation, he condemned the government's failure to embrace full citizenship for freed slaves.

Democrats hated him. Hodgson mocked Hickman's fraternizing with his "woolly-headed [African American] brudders." On the grounds of the U.S. Capitol, a southern congressman took a swing at him.

"He did not seek an early political life," said fellow attorney William Darlington on the occasion of Hickman's death. "But having entered into its

Disaffected Democrat John Hickman helped form the Chester County Republican Party after splitting with the leaders of his party over slavery. The editor of a Democratic newspaper called him little better than "a Black Republican." *Library of Congress.*

arena, he devoted his characteristic vim to its work, and may well be said to have always proved himself a true representative of the people who rallied to his standard."

Born in West Bradford Township, Hickman was the son of farmers John and Sarah Hickman. The Hickmans apparently valued education because they hired a private tutor who drilled their boy in the classics and mathematics. Hickman at first planned to become a physician but could not endure the required hours in the dissecting rooms. He next considered the ministry but eventually settled on law. Admitted to the bar in 1834, he spent the following ten years building a practice.

In 1844, Hickman got his first taste of politics. He offered himself to local Democrats as a candidate for Congress but lost the nomination to a more established party member. Perhaps as a consolation, Hickman was sent as a delegate to that year's national convention, which nominated Democrat James K. Polk for president.

It was the age of Jackson. Beginning with the election of Andrew Jackson in 1828, the Democratic Party—usually headed by land-hungry southerners—had led the nation on a thirty-year expansion spree. The Cherokee and Choctaw tribes were evicted from their lands in the Deep South. The country confronted Great Britain over the country's northwest border and walked away with Oregon and Washington. Under Polk, the United States would seize the entire Southwest and California from Mexico.

All of this land grabbing suited the national mood, except in the effete Northeast, where the Whig Party ruled. The Whigs' priorities were internal improvements, public schools and protective tariffs—a platform supported by business and financial interests and the growing antislavery movement. The Know-Nothings had similar domestic interests, plus a dislike for immigrants. The Northeast had little interest in additional real estate that would have to be defended and developed on its own—and much of which would become slave territory anyway.

"In the murder of Mexicans upon their own soil, or in robbing them of their country, I can take no part," said Joshua Giddings (1795–1864), an Ohio Whig who voted against troops and weapons for the Mexican-American War. "The guilt of these crimes must rest on others." To Democrats, this disinterest in empire on the part of northeastern Whigs marked both their region and their party as a little girly, if not treasonous.

Whigs aside, the country was in the hands of a coalition of northern and southern Democrats, held together by agreements to give each section some of what it wanted and to leave the South alone about slavery. Northern Democrats, who often shared the distaste for slavery of their Whig and Know-Nothing neighbors, were accustomed to holding their noses for party unity.

At the 1844 convention, the issue was Texas. Independent since 1836, Texas had first petitioned to be admitted as a state in 1837. Martin Van Buren, president from 1837 to 1841, rejected the request rather than risk war with Mexico. His successor, John Tyler (president, 1841–45) favored annexation, but the Senate did not approve. A majority of Democrats came to the convention favoring annexation, but the leading candidate was Van Buren, who did not. Long story short, the pro-southern, proslavery, prowar side muscled Van Buren aside and nominated Polk, who was elected.

Annexation and war followed.

Surely impressed with the power of proslavery Democrats, Hickman came home to consider his future in the party. In 1845, he was appointed district attorney for Chester County, serving for fifteen months. Subsequently, he was chair of the state Democratic Central Committee. Both were handy spots to park and ripen an up-and-comer. In 1854, Hickman tried again for Congress and was elected.

Party leaders may have thought that they had a regular, toe-the-line Democrat in Sixth District freshman John Hickman. Critics would later charge that—like former U.S. senator Arlen Specter of Pennsylvania—Hickman's political independence was more opportunistic than principled. Hodgson sneered that Hickman had merely gotten bored with the law and was lusting for a $3,000 congressional salary.

Hickman's independence became plain in 1855 when he refused to support his party's choice, South Carolinian William Aiken, for Speaker of the House against Nathaniel P. Banks (R-Massachusetts). Hickman voted for an obscure Democrat instead.

It was not a minor issue. The House was narrowly divided between slave and free states. Throwing the speakership to one side or the other would affect the balance of power. Banks was a leading opponent of the Kansas-Nebraska Act, which had opened territory above the Mason-Dixon line to slavery.

"The handful of votes from northern Democrats like Hickman, who refused to be dictated to by the South, cost Aiken the speakership," wrote historian Douglas R. Harper.

Banks took the gavel.

Back in Chester County, Hickman was damned as a party traitor. Hodgson raged that Hickman and another local congressman "threw away their votes. These two votes would have elected the Democratic candidate and defeated Banks."

However, many local Democrats weren't upset at all. They didn't like slavery either and were tired of being dictated to by the South. Whigs and Know-Nothings, meanwhile, were positively pleased. According to Harper, Northerners generally were disgusted with their elected leaders in the 1850s. In particular, they were upset over the Fugitive Slave Act, which required local authorities to help capture runaways. Suddenly, they could see the face of slavery right here in the neighborhood.

Hickman, however, had offended entrenched Washington politicians, so the home folks loved him. He was reelected in 1856 as a Democrat with quiet support from Whigs and Know-Nothings. It was a good year for the Pennsylvania party because James Buchanan of Lancaster was running for president. Publicly, Hickman supported Buchanan and the Democratic platform but, as a bitter Hodgson complained, did not campaign for either.

"To preserve harmony and union, the Democrats of Chester acceded to the [Hickman] nomination and from that time to the October election, Mr. Hickman was busy making some of his 50 speeches," wrote the *Jeffersonian* editor, "not for Mr. Buchanan, but for himself."

As president, the Democrat Buchanan leaned predictably south. He is believed to have lobbied a U.S. Supreme Court justice to vote with Chief

Justice Roger B. Taney on the *Dred Scott* decision that Congress had no right to exclude slavery from the territories. Buchanan also favored the admission of Kansas as a slave state under the so-called Lecompton Constitution written by the proslavery side. (Proslavery and antislavery settlers in that state were fighting a low-grade civil war at the time.)

Hickman was a vehement anti-Lecompton Democrat. In early 1858, Hodgson, the *Jeffersonian* editor, practically frothed when he described an impromptu Hickman appearance on the post office steps "surrounded by scores of Black Republicans attracted by his anti-Lecompton ravings about the 'tyranny of the South,' 'cowardly rascals and doughfaces of the North' and other Abolition lingo." (Black Republicans weren't African American. Hodgson used the adjective as a synonym for evil, dangerous or "nigger loving.")

Two years earlier, campaigning as a Democrat, Hickman had dismissed as "traitors to the Union and the Constitution" the abolitionists who now cheered him. Now, something had to change. The Democrats moved first. In 1858, the party nominated a different candidate for Congress.

A few weeks later, Hickman walked up High Street to a mass meeting of the disenchanted—Democrats, Whigs and Know-Nothings—plus members of the still-forming Republican Party. There, he was praised by the likes of William Whitehead, a Republican and abolitionist whom Hickman had defeated in 1854.

"I never voted for, never supported him," said Whitehead. "But when I now see him an exponent of my principles, I am bound to sustain him." Whitehead was not alone. Another attendee said flatly, "Hickman made Kansas free." In October, Hickman was elected as an independent. He had carried nearly half of Democratic voters and large majorities of those from other parties. By 1860, when Hickman ran again as a Republican, those other parties had disappeared.

All of this meant that, a year later, Hickman was still on the House floor to declare that the North would never permit secession. "How will you prevent it?" came the taunting reply of Georgia representative—and future Confederate general—Lucius Jeremiah Gantrell.

"I will tell you how it can be prevented," replied Hickman. "With all the appliances of art to assist, 18 million men, reared to industry, with habits of the right kind, will always be able to cope successfully with eight million men without these auxiliaries."

Hickman's fellow Republicans cheered. The Democrats hissed.

1862

BURYING TOM BELL

Any discussion of military funerals usually comes down to respect. No one feels that there can be too much. That's why the media remains restricted in its coverage of returning war casualties and why so many find demonstrators at funerals so infuriating.

But really, why respect the military dead at all?

It wasn't always this way. Punctiliousness about the corpses of U.S. soldiers can be traced to the Civil War, when only a few were treated as tenderly as Lieutenant Colonel Thomas S. Bell (1838–1862) of West Chester. Bell, a young lawyer and one of the town's favorite sons, was killed at the Battle of Antietam. Three days later, on September 20, Bell's uncle and a friend received his body at the West Chester train station. There, they pried open the rough coffin—hammered together on the battlefield by Bell's comrades—and looked inside.

Their reaction? Ewwwww.

"Decay's effacing fingers have been busily at work marring the lineaments of his fine face and features," reported the *Village Record* newspaper. What to do? A public funeral had been announced for the following day, and tradition required the presence of a corpse. Still, the icky facts were undeniable. Bell's remains were taken straight to Oaklands Cemetery.

In that era, most of the nation's used-up cannon fodder were simply shoveled into pits or left to rot. Burial details, observed one Union chaplain, covered bodies "much the same as farmers cover potatoes…with this exception, however: the vegetables really get more tender care." Many went into the ground naked, stripped by those desperate for clothing and shoes.

Killed at Antietam, Colonel Thomas S. Bell of West Chester was luckier than most men who died in the Civil War: he got a (crude) coffin and a marked grave. Dead enlisted men were often thrown into trenches or even left to rot. *Library of Congress.*

Such tales shocked a nation in which a "good death" happened at home, in old age and surrounded by family and then was followed by religious services and burial in a local graveyard.

"Perhaps the most distressing aspect of death for many Civil War Americans was that thousands of young men were dying away from home," wrote historian Drew Gilpin Faust. "But the four years of civil war overturned conventions and expectations."

Born in West Chester, Bell was the son and namesake of a prominent local judge. Thomas S. Bell Sr. had moved in 1821 from Philadelphia to Chester County to practice law. In 1837, he was elected to represent Chester and Montgomery Counties at the state constitutional convention. Later, he served in the state senate and, for five years, on the state supreme court. By 1859, the year in which his son was admitted to the Chester County Bar,

Judge Bell had returned to private practice. Father and son discussed going into practice together.

Young Tom Bell was raised in a house that still stands at Church and Miner Streets. Educated at the West Chester Academy (now West Chester University), he studied law in his father's office. Bell joined the county militia in 1858 and ran unsuccessfully for the state legislature in 1860. Public spirited and ambitious, he was among the first to respond when President Lincoln called for volunteers to put down the rebellion.

"Do try, my dearest father, to keep up your spirits," Bell wrote from Camp Curtin near Harrisburg in April 1861. "I am going in a just cause and the almighty arm that protects us in peace will not be withdrawn from me in the crash of battle."

Brave words, but Bell spent his initial enlistment doing nothing much. The Civil War was expected to be short, so early volunteers signed up for only three months. Bell's unit, the Ninth Pennsylvania Volunteers, was mustered in April and discharged in July.

But that was enough time for Bell to demonstrate his character. When another regiment rioted after receiving hardtack rather than bread, for instance, Bell reacted quickly.

"I was aroused by shouts in the street and found about half of the 11th [Regiment] shouting, 'crackers,' 'Lincoln flints,' 'give us the Commissary,' etc.," Bell wrote home. "I went out amongst them, found they were disposed to raise a difficulty and so hurried off and got four companies, marched with them and arrested all men not in charge of an officer…Thank fortune the 9th didn't disgrace itself by taking part."

Subsequently ordered to Delaware to intimidate local secessionists, the Ninth finished its service in northern Virginia, where the green armies mostly sat and watched each other. But when a Confederate scouting party spooked a superior officer, Bell's account dripped with contempt. "[The rebels] advanced pickets on a hill, whereupon he retreated with his staff back to the wagons, called upon his officers to close around him in single file and sent forward for a company 'for God's sake to come back and defend them,'" wrote Bell. "Girl! He should be dressed in a ribbed petticoat and sent home."

Bell immediately reenlisted in the new three-year Fifty-first Pennsylvania and then suffered "the blues" as he waited weeks for it to depart.

"To be inactive now makes me…so sad and gloomy that I've been a burden to myself," he wrote in September. "I feel that I must have made my presence far from pleasant to my friends. Before long, I hope to feel very differently."

Promoted to lieutenant colonel, Bell with the Fifty-first joined Ambrose Burnside's assault on a rebel fort at New Bern, North Carolina. Advancing from transports on the Neuse River in March 1862, the Fifty-first exchanged one volley with the Confederates. Then Bell ordered his men to charge.

"To you, I don't mind confessing that after this my recollection is very confused," Bell wrote home. "I only remember rushing down the hill [and] struggling through broken timbers and water. How I got on their breastworks I don't yet know." The rebels fled, and the region remained under Union control throughout the war.

That summer, the Fifty-first participated in the disastrous Second Battle of Bull Run, after which the defeated Union army fled to the defenses of Washington. As an emboldened Robert E. Lee planned his first invasion of the Northern states, Lincoln again put General George B. McClellan in charge. This pleased the army, including Bell. His final letter told his family not to worry.

"They will never enter Chester County," wrote Bell on September 10. "And if they venture to cross into Pennsylvania, I'd stake almost anything that a battle would soon be fought that would forever crush them." By this time, though, Lee's army was already north of the Potomac.

On September 14, Bell and the Fifty-first were at the Battle of South Mountain, where McClellan seized three passes that his army had to control to reach Lee. That night, in his characteristic one-eighth-inch script, Bell made his last diary entry, writing that "the action was kept up…until about 8 p.m., when the fire slackened and stopped. We lay in the woods behind the wall, watching the right all night."

Three days later, McClellan's army met Lee's troops, lined up along Antietam Creek. Bell and the Fifty-first were ordered to attack across a narrow stone bridge. Confederate cannons responded with grapeshot, a form of ammunition consisting of dozens of 1.5-inch iron balls that sprayed out like shotgun pellets.

One ball hit Bell behind the left ear. "I don't think it is dangerous," Bell told Sergeant Edwin Bennett, who was among the first to reach him. "Boys, never say die." But Bell did die, at about 5:00 p.m. in a nearby farmhouse.

When the Civil War began, there was little preparation for medical care and almost none for burying the dead. Hospitals were required to bury those who died in their care. But when the armies were in the field, care of the dead was usually the responsibility of a soldier's friends.

That worked when soldiers died by ones and twos. But at Antietam, twenty-three thousand men lay dead or wounded, along with countless horses and mules. A week later, Dr. Daniel M. Holt, a Union army surgeon, reported that "the dead were almost wholly unburied, and the stench arising from it was such as to breed a pestilence."

In one place, wrote Holt, he saw "stretched along, in one straight line, ready for interment, at least a thousand blackened, bloated corpses with blood and gas protruding from every orifice, and maggots holding high carnival over their heads."

Assignment to burial detail was often a punishment. In any case, it was a chore that soldiers wanted to finish quickly and by touching the bodies as little as possible. One technique was to loop a rope around the feet and then use a bent bayonet to drag corpses to a burial site. One Union burial party threw fifty-eight dead Confederates down a well.

Officers got better treatment, as is shown by the shipment home of Bell's body. After the 1862 Battle of Cedar Mountain, noted historian Faust, most Union dead lay on the battlefield for days. The exceptions were their dead officers, who were gathered up, packed in charcoal, placed in metal coffins and sent by train to their homes across the north.

Such differences annoyed the troops. As a Texas soldier put it, "The officers get the honor; you get nothing. They get a monument; you get a hole in the ground and no coffin." Overall, Civil War soldiers accepted the possibility of death—a subject to which, according to Faust, they devoted much thought, in part to avoid thinking about their role in the killing. But they hated that they might be chewed on by wild animals. As he lay dying at Gettysburg, for instance, Jeremiah Gage of the Eleventh Mississippi asked "to be buried like my comrades. But deep, boys, deep, so the beasts won't get me."

Entrepreneurial traveling undertakers who followed the armies tried to fill the void. But even this market-based solution was unable to keep up with the universal desire for a coffin, shipment home and burial in a marked grave. The solution was to create battlefield cemeteries—Gettysburg, Antietam and others—where all would receive a measure of the respect given Tom Bell. Battlefield cemeteries, in turn, eventually spawned a desire for military cemeteries for all veterans and their families, as well as their attendant rituals.

Since we still haven't seen fit to stop the killing, it remains the best we can do.

1863

War Changes Things

War makes people do things that they would not do otherwise. Not all of them are unspeakable.

In 1863, for instance, the men of the Ninety-seventh Pennsylvania Volunteer Infantry—a regiment raised in Chester and Delaware Counties—risked their lives for others in danger. The Ninety-seventh was white. The others, wounded survivors of the Fifty-fourth Massachusetts "Glory" regiment, were black. And for that fact alone, they were in particular danger as they lay bleeding in front of Confederate Fort Wagner.

Union brigadier general Thomas G. Stevenson (1836–1864) framed the issue plainly. "You know," he told the men of the Ninety-seventh, "how much harder *they* will fare at the hands of the enemy than white men." The Pennsylvanians, then, worked through the night, under fire, to get the Fifty-fourth's wounded into ambulances.

Blacks in Pennsylvania also had it harder than whites. But until that moment in the siege of Charleston, South Carolina, few in the Ninety-seventh had likely ever been personally called on to act on it.

The Ninety-seventh was raised primarily by Henry R. Guss (1825–1907), an entrepreneur who had been active in the local militia since he joined the National Guards of West Chester at the age of twenty-one. In civilian life, Guss operated a tavern, the Green Tree Hotel, from 1854 to 1892, as well as a brickyard. He also seems to have been a man who, at least for his time, was without obvious racial prejudice. In 1907, in announcing his death, the *Daily Local News* reported that "[m]any colored men and their families, who formerly were in the employ of Gen. Guss, or who knew him personally, will likely call and they will be welcome."

After the black Fifty-fourth Massachusetts Regiment's failed attack on Fort Wagner in 1863, the Ninety-seventh Pennsylvania Volunteer Infantry—seen here at a postwar reunion—took up the task of rescuing its wounded. *Chester County Historical Society.*

A regular employer-employee relationship was above average in a state in which African Americans were severely handicapped by prejudice. Though a "free" state, the Pennsylvania constitution of 1838 denied blacks the right to vote. (The previous constitution had not done this.) Official discrimination sanctioned private prejudice, and over time, African Americans lost access to the artisanal and professional jobs to which they had been rising. Thereafter, most black men here could find jobs only as day laborers.

Guss was promoted, in 1854, to lieutenant and, in 1859, to captain (commanding officer). In 1861, he was commissioned as a colonel with authority to enlist men willing to fight for the duration of the war.

He enlisted 950. Three of the regiment's eleven companies—the Concordville Rifles, the Broomall Guards and the Brooke Guards—signed up in Delaware County, with the remaining eight companies from Chester County. But the men themselves came from everywhere. The largest contingent, 15 percent (143 men), was from West Chester; Coatesville was second at 5 percent (45 men). But volunteers also came from Berks, Lancaster, York and Montgomery Counties and from Philadelphia. Enlistees also came from Maryland, Massachusetts, New York and Rhode Island and included recent immigrants from Ireland, Germany and Switzerland. One-third were farmers. Others were carpenters and blacksmiths, and many were common laborers. The average age was twenty-two, but the drummer boy was twelve.

"We will never know what motivated each of these men to volunteer," wrote historian Keith Doms, who studied Ninety-seventh demographics. "It is likely that many volunteered as a patriotic act. For others, it was a chance for a grand adventure."

The regiment trained at Camp Wayne, now part of the West Chester University campus, and accepted the adoration of the town. Friends of Company C brought 101 pair of socks. Members of Company A were deluged with edibles. A Methodist minister brought Bibles. The governor visited to present the regiment's official flag. In November, when the Ninety-seventh marched to the West Chester depot, "The murmur of thousands of voices mingled in last adieus found at length its culmination, breaking forth in hearty cheers for the boys in blue," according to regimental historian (and dentist) Isaiah Price.

In Georgia, the Ninety-seventh helped capture Fort Pulaski; in Florida, it occupied Jacksonville and St. Augustine. In June 1862, the regiment took part in an unsuccessful attempt to capture Charleston by land and then joined hundreds of other Union regiments in continual skirmishing around the city. In one such engagement, Price recalled Guss riding back and forth in front of his men, urging them to remain steady.

"His example was electric in its effect," wrote Price, "for the men were rendered cool and brave by the coolness and bravery of their commander himself, in the thickest of the danger."

The men of the Fifty-fourth, in contrast, had to fight just for the right to fight.

Despite intense pressure from both black leaders and abolitionists who thought that allowing blacks to serve would cement their right to liberty, the government did not authorize such enlistments until January 1863. And then the Lincoln administration insulted its new black troops by deciding—despite initial promises—that black troops would be paid only seven dollars per month (ten dollars, minus three dollars for clothing). White troops earned thirteen dollars and did not have to pay for their uniforms. In protest, the Fifty-fourth refused for eighteen months to accept any pay until—after many battles and casualties—Congress passed an "equalization" law.

"We should not have it said," asserted Sergeant William Gray, "that knowing our rights we did not stand up for them."

The regiment totaled 1,100 men. Some came from communities of fugitive slaves in Canada, but most were born free. Others came from New

Guarded by African American troops in 1865, Confederate Fort Wagner protected Charleston against federal assault. From the Union perspective, Wagner had to go. *Library of Congress.*

York and Pennsylvania. The Fifty-fourth's white officers were selected from the families of wealthy abolitionists who could be counted on to finance the outfitting of such troops. (One backer, ship chandler George Stearns, had also helped fund John Brown.) Among the enlistees were two sons of Frederick Douglass who, in a newspaper editorial, called the nation's black men to arms: "We can get at the throat of treason and slavery through the State of Massachusetts."

Nevertheless, in May 1863 most Bostonians who watched were impressed as Colonel Robert Gould Shaw marched the Fifty-fourth down Beacon Street to the strains of "John Brown's Body"—a scene now memorialized in bronze on Boston Common. (Exceptions were the street thugs who assaulted the rear of the column as it boarded the steamer taking the Fifty-fourth south.)

By July, both the Ninety-seventh and Fifty-fourth were among three brigades (fourteen regiments) facing Battery Wagner, a Confederate fort erected to defend Charleston. The Fifty-fourth was among six regiments in a brigade commanded by Brigadier General George Strong; the Ninety-seventh was one of four regiments in a brigade led by Stevenson. Another brigade of four regiments was led by Colonel Haldimand Putnam.

Battery Wagner measured 100 by 250 yards and was located on a flat beach 100 yards from the Atlantic with a moat in its front and a swamp in its rear. Constructed of palmetto logs and sandbags, it was defended by 1,700 soldiers and fourteen cannons. Union ships approaching Charleston would be caught between Wagner and rebel-occupied Fort Sumter in the harbor. Wagner had to go.

Somehow, the Union command decided that infantry could overwhelm the fort. Putnam called it suicidal and remarked to a fellow officer, "We are going into Wagner like a flock of sheep." But Strong agreed with the strategy, and perhaps for that reason, his brigade was chosen to lead the attack. Strong put the Fifty-fourth in front.

On July 18, Union ships bombarded Wagner all day. The expectation was that this would leave the fort so shattered and the Confederates so dazed that a nighttime infantry attack would be successful. But the fort wasn't badly damaged, and Wagner's garrison had been well sheltered.

As night fell, Shaw told his men, "I want you to prove yourselves. The eyes of thousands will look on what you do tonight."

Casualties in the Fifty-fourth were 42 percent. "The rebs withheld their fire until we reached within 50 yards of the work," wrote George E. Stephens, the Fifty-fourth's black historian, "when jets of flame darted forth from every corner and embrasure." Of the 600 members of the regiment who participated in the attack, 54 were killed or received mortal wounds. Another 52 were missing, and 149 were left wounded, many lying on the sand around the rebel fort. White troops coming up behind the Fifty-fourth also suffered heavy casualties. Shaw died on Wagner's parapet and was later reported by the rebels to have been buried facedown "with his niggers." Outraged at having to fight blacks, the Confederates bayoneted some captured soldiers and refused a truce that would have allowed the wounded to be gathered.

Meanwhile, the Ninety-seventh and the rest of Stevenson's brigade had waited in reserve to back up the attack if it had proved successful. When it became plain that this wouldn't be necessary, Stevenson called for three Ninety-seventh companies—led by Guss, Captain Dewitt Lewis (a West Chester carpenter) and Lieutenant Colonel A.P. Duer, a West Point graduate who later served as Chester County sheriff—to give covering fire. Four other companies stacked arms and began to gather the wounded.

Ironically, Stevenson, a Massachusetts officer, had publicly opposed enlisting or serving with blacks. However, his promotion to brigadier that year was endorsed by abolitionist Senator Charles Sumner (R-Massachusetts), and Stevenson later said that African Americans were good soldiers. He was killed the following year at Spotsylvania Courthouse.

"The search for the wounded," wrote Price, "was pushed to the moat and slopes of the fort by our men, who lay on the ground and crept along under cover of darkness, listening for the groans of the wounded as a guide to find them." Stevenson, wrote Price, was "particularly anxious that every wounded colored soldier should be brought off." Not all were; some wounded lying near the ocean drowned when the tide came in.

Throughout, Confederate snipers and artillery were active. According to Price, this so concerned the ambulance drivers (not members of the Ninety-seventh) "as to cause them to start off their teams at a run as soon as their load of wounded soldiers was ready, regardless of the piercing cries of the poor suffers." An officer of the Ninety-seventh, presumably Guss, stopped this by putting a guard on each ambulance with orders to shoot the driver if he broke out of a walk.

"It was a sad and anxious night's work," wrote Price, "never to be forgotten by those engaged in bearing off the fallen ones from that thickly strewn field."

1866

Ceasing to Blush

Bigots are always their own worst enemies.

In 1861, they married the cause of slavery—an ancient, constitutionally protected institution—to secession. (Dumb.) In the early 1960s, they turned fire hoses on peaceful demonstrators *while TV cameras were watching*! (Dumb.)

They were also dumb in 1869. That was the year in which Chester County's Dr. Ann Preston (1813–1872), dean of the Woman's Medical College of Pennsylvania—the first such institution in the world—led her female students into a lab at Pennsylvania Hospital. The reaction?

"The male medical students shouted insults and threw paper, tinfoil, and tobacco quids," wrote historian Margaret Hope Bacon. "The female medical students remained composed and attended the clinic, but on their way out they were pelted with rocks."

Even in that misogynistic era, one didn't publicly insult or throw rocks at women. The incident discredited the most outspoken opponents of female physicians and helped stiffen the spines of their supporters.

And today? Female applicants to U.S. medical schools slightly outnumber men.

For the Woman's Medical College, "Preston exemplified woman as leader," wrote historian Stephen Jay Peitzman. "Nothing appeared in the college's promotional literature more often than images of Preston, into which the viewer imaginatively reads strength and resolve."

The youngest of nine children born to Quaker farmers Amos and Margaret (Smith) Preston, Ann Preston grew up at Prestonville, a Londongrove farm purchased in 1785 by her grandfather. She attended a neighborhood

Women like these in an 1870 anatomy lab will suffer for knowing too much, said those who opposed training women to be physicians. "Will woman gain by ceasing to blush?" asked the Philadelphia Medical Society. *Library of Congress.*

school and, briefly, a boarding school in West Chester. But after her mother sickened, Preston became her nurse and inherited the chores that came with helping raise six older brothers.

"Nothing from the first 37 years of Ann Preston's life suggests that she was interested in medicine, let alone that she would become dean of a medical school," wrote historian Susan Wells.

Nothing outwardly, that is. Inwardly, Preston could not miss that—besides a chronically ill mother—her family included three daughters. Both of her sisters died in childhood, although all of her brothers survived. Later, Preston would connect female mortality to sedentary, indoor occupations and restrictive clothing.

Preston's early letters reveal her interest in literature, current events and politics, fed by the local Farmers' Library, a lyceum visited by famous speakers and a literary society.

"Every American female has and should feel a deep interest in the welfare of her country," wrote Preston to her friend, Hannah Darlington, in 1835. "If she feels no interest in the perpetuation and perfection of republican freedom, half of the support of our government is lost."

In 1869, Dr. Ann Preston of Chester County led her female students into a lab at Pennsylvania Hospital only to be met by a hail of "paper, tinfoil, and tobacco quids" from hostile male students. That under-fire episode made Preston a hero to generations of students at the Woman's Medical College of Pennsylvania. *Library of Congress.*

By modern standards, the Prestons trended left. When an 1827 schism divided area Quakers, the family went with the liberal Hicksites, who emphasized continuing revelation over the Bible. The Prestons were abolitionists, and their daughter came early to that cause.

It is telling that Preston joined the Clarkson Anti-Slavery Society, a Quaker organization based in Chester and Lancaster Counties that accepted men and women on an equal basis. Most antislavery organizations accepted only men, requiring women to observe from the sidelines.

The Clarkson group was radical in other ways. In 1840, it vehemently criticized a proposal by the older Chester County Abolitionist Society that every black male pay a head tax to "finance the passage of free Negroes to Liberia." Hypocrisy, thundered the Clarksonites, whose letters to the editor condemned the "pretended compassion" of those who were "as bad as the slaveholders."

As Clarkson secretary, Preston was responsible for writing and distributing such statements. She also circulated a petition against capital punishment and agitated on behalf of an anti-tavern bill that, she hoped, would "let the rumsellers feel insecure in their nefarious business."

In 1838, Preston traveled to Philadelphia with friends for dedication ceremonies at Pennsylvania Hall, a new antislavery meeting place on Sixth Street. Instead, she witnessed the building's destruction by a proslavery mob. In a letter, Preston described the event as an "awful and grand spectacle" though not a discouraging one.

"I have heard of some abolitionists whose faith has been shaken by recent events, but I have met with none such," she wrote to Darlington. "All… seem determined to persevere with renewed energy." Preston's poem "The Burning of Pennsylvania Hall" was chosen from among several hundred to be published in a book about the event:

> *Oh! Slavery's form that hour was seen*
> *Polluting all our air*
> *Its fearful front and fiendish mien*
> *And twining chains were bare*
> *And well that hall, in freedom's name*
> *Hath spoken out with words of flame!*

After her siblings grew up, Preston taught school and wrote rhymed tales for children, published as *Cousin Ann's Stories* in 1849. Most taught simple morals such as neatness and kindness. But others emphasized temperance or antislavery ideas. In "Howard and His Squirrel," a boy frees a caged pet:

> *But Howard thought he should not like*
> *a little slave to be*
> *and God had made the nimble squirrel*
> *to run and climb the tree.*

Never married, Preston may initially have been attracted to political activity, at least in part, by simple boredom. Many of her early letters are laments to girlhood friends who had married and no longer had time for her.

"I always had an idea that when persons got married they changed," Preston wrote in 1833 to Hannah Monaghan Darlington, who had recently married and moved to Kennett Square, "that instead of the noble generous feelings of earlier times they became selfish and contracted, and loved nothing outside of their own doors."

But by 1843, she was the busy one. "How I wish thee was an abolitionist," she wrote to Lavinia Passmore, another girlhood friend. "I should then get to see thee at least at anti-slavery meetings."

In 1847, encouraged by Philadelphia Quakers interested in medical education for women, Preston enrolled as an apprentice in the office of Dr. Nathaniel Moseley. After two years, she applied to medical colleges but was turned down because of her gender.

Meanwhile, local physicians and philanthropists had been busily organizing the Female Medical College. Among them was Dr. Joseph S. Longshore, a Quaker obstetrician who, like Preston, thought it simply wrong that women should be ignorant of their own bodies. Galvanized by the 1848 graduation of Elizabeth Blackwell from a medical school in Syracuse, New York, Longshore and his allies submitted incorporation papers to the state legislature, which approved in March 1850.

In August, the founders rented space on Arch Street and began to recruit faculty. (Most local physicians refused to have anything to do with this radical new enterprise.) In October, forty students—including Preston—were greeted by six faculty, including Moseley. By the following January (1851), she was enthusiastically immersed in her studies and predicting the school's success, despite constant obstacles.

"There is a considerable and increasing apparatus and the professors...have their hearts in their business," she wrote to Darlington. "[But] Dr. Moseley...was lately proposed as an honorary member of the Philadelphia Medical Society solely, as it appears, for the purpose of blackballing him, which was done...[as a] gratituitous insult because of his connection with a female college."

Preston graduated with the first class. She spent a year in Paris, studying obstetrics at the Maternite Hospital and, upon her return, was hired to be the college's professor of physiology and hygiene. In 1866, she was named dean of the college faculty, a position she held until her death. Simultaneously, Preston maintained a medical practice and made house calls.

"I called on Mrs. Lane in a splendid house in Girard Street," she wrote Darlington in 1854, "and only a few rods distant in an alley forlorn and filthy, I called on Mrs. Robinson, a poor patient, my wash woman. Ah, what suffering and poverty there is in this city!"

Preston's students also needed such experience, but all city hospitals were closed to them. So, she founded a new one. Preston found a site facing Girard College and then undertook the fundraising herself. She walked door to door in the city and then borrowed a buggy and drove farm to farm in Bucks, Chester and Montgomery Counties.

"Slowly the money trickled in," wrote Bacon. "One wonderful day, a farmer gave her the last hundred dollars she needed, and she drove back to the city thanking God for the fulfillment of her dream." The Woman's Hospital of Philadelphia opened in 1862.

Feeling threatened, the Philadelphia Medical Society in 1867 forbade its members from consulting with any female physician. "It is sufficient," read the society's resolution, "to allude merely to the embarrassments which would be encountered on both sides in her visiting and prescribing for persons of the opposite sex. Will woman gain by ceasing to blush while discussing every topic?"

In biting reply, Preston noted that women had already seen it all. In every society throughout time, she wrote, women tended every cradle and sickbed "with a power of sustained endurance that man does not claim to possess."

The Woman's Medical Hospital merged with West Philadelphia Hospital for Women in 1929 and then with the Hospital of the University of Pennsylvania in 1964. Female Medical College became the Woman's Medical College in 1867 and the Medical College of Pennsylvania (MCP) in 1970, and in 1993 it merged with Hahnemann University to become MCP Hahnemann School of Medicine. Since 2002, it has been part of the Drexel School of Medicine.

Preston remained the hero of Woman's Medical College long after her death. In the early twentieth century, an 1889 graduate who never knew Preston personally recalled a cherished institutional memory: "The story of Dr. Ann Preston, the first dean of the College, leading a small group of women medical students in forced march down the middle of Chestnut Street protected by the police from a mob of male medical students."

Pray, gentlemen, that your female physician is thinking of something else at your next prostate exam.

1866

MARY MILES'S LONG RIDE

Beware of unintended consequences. Do the right thing and, sometimes, the result can be very wrong.

Consider, for instance, Mary E. Miles, an African American woman from Chester County who—like Rosa Parks—refused to move to the black seats on a Philadelphia-to-Oxford train in the spring of 1866. She eventually won the right to sit where she pleased. In the process, though, Miles created a legal precedent that oppressed blacks until the civil rights era.

Little is known of Miles's early life. Born free in Philadelphia, she was a teacher who worked among the freedmen for years. From the late 1850s until the mid-1860s, she served in Africa as a missionary with her husband, whose name was probably James. In 1865, due to his ill health, they sailed for home, but he died in England.

In 1866, Miles applied for a teaching position with the Friends Freedmen's Association (FFA), a Quaker group that sent teachers into the Reconstruction South to teach freed slaves. When her court case was reported the following year, the *National Anti-Slavery Standard* newspaper described her as "a woman of education and refinement." Finally hired by FFA in 1869, she taught until 1875 in Virginia and North Carolina.

Waiting for her FFA appointment, Miles taught locally and seems to have lived at Hinsonville, a rural community of free blacks that became the site of Lincoln University. Hinsonville was part of a belt of black settlements that stretched from West Philadelphia through places such as Darby, Morton and Media to Kennett Square and beyond.

Commuting between Philadelphia and her home near this station in 1866, Mary Miles decided—like Rosa Parks almost a century later—that she would not move to the black section of the train. *Dolores Rowe.*

When Miles arrived home from Africa, slavery was no longer the primary civil rights issue. That was dying along with the Confederacy. Instead, practical-minded activists were demanding equal access to streetcars and trolleys, which were the only way for many blacks to reach their jobs.

African Americans had always worked on the railroads. In the South, slaves had provided most of the manpower to build and operate the lines. In Pennsylvania, the first African American was hired in 1840 by the Philadelphia & Columbia to handle baggage. Many others followed, mostly working in similar support jobs as porters, passenger car attendants, dining car chefs and waiters.

Riding as a passenger was another matter. Beginning in the 1840s, blacks were segregated if they were lucky and banned if they weren't. Austrian engineer Franz Ritter von Gerstner, who visited the United States from 1838 to 1840, found segregation in both the South and the North. On the Baltimore & Susquehanna Railroad, which ran from Baltimore to York, he recorded an eight-wheel baggage car with three sections—one for luggage, one for "latrines" and one for "Negroes."

Blacks had few ways way to resist; revision of the state constitution in 1838 had deprived them of the right to vote. Black children were even excluded temporarily from some public schools. (Robert Purvis got one such decision reversed when he refused to pay his property taxes.)

Perhaps because their cars were smaller and more intimate, local trolley and streetcar operators were more likely to prohibit black passengers. Access to these lines was also more essential to daily life, however, and protests began before the Civil War. In 1864, coal merchant William Still used a support-the-troops strategy to argue that the policies harmed wounded veterans in West Philadelphia army hospitals.

"The 1,500 wounded soldiers…at the Summit and Satterlee hospitals received but few visits from their colored brethren, simply because the rules enforced on these cars would not allow decent colored people to ride," wrote Still in 1864. "The presence and succor of such mother, wife or sister might save a life."

In Harrisburg, abolitionists led by State Senator Morrow B. Lowry introduced a bill in 1865 prohibiting "any passenger railway company [from] excluding any race of people from its passenger cars on account of color." The bill would pass, but not until 1867. In 1866, activist Octavius Catto launched an organized protest in which white supporters boycotted the cars or—on lines that allowed blacks to ride, but only outside with the driver—stood with them on exterior platforms. "Our dear friend, Lucretia Mott, now so ill, has taken her stand beside them in that exposed position," wrote Alfred H. Love to the *National Anti-Slavery Standard* newspaper in 1867.

In this environment, Miles walked one day into the Philadelphia depot of the West Chester & Philadelphia Railroad (WC&PR) at Thirty-first and Chestnut. The WC&PR, with a spur that ran from Wawa west through Chadds Ford, Kennett Square and on to Hinsonville, was a relatively progressive company. Blacks were allowed to ride though were required to sit in a separate section. Miles paid for her ticket and took a seat.

The details of what happened next have not survived. Miles would later sue in Philadelphia Orphan's Court, but most of that court's older records were discarded in the mid-1980s. The short version is that Miles was put off the train. This might have happened before it left the station or perhaps somewhere in Delaware County.

The Pennsylvania Supreme Court decision stated that Miles took a seat in the middle of the car. The conductor reminded her of company rules that she sit at the end of the car. "She declined positively and persistently to do it," said the court. "The conductor…warned her that he must require her to leave the cars if she refused, and at last put her out."

And then there was this curious sentence. "There was no allegation," according to the decision, "that any force was used greater than was necessary to accomplish the object of compelling her to leave the cars." (This begs the question: how much force was *that?*)

Miles sued WC&PR for "trespass" (assault, essentially) for forcing her from the train and charged that any rule "which prohibits a well-behaved colored person from taking a vacant seat…is not a regulation which the law allows." The court agreed and awarded Miles five dollars in damages. But the railroad appealed and won before the state supreme court.

The decision was read by Chief Justice Daniel Agnew (1809–1902), a native of Trenton, New Jersey, who had lived in Mississippi as a child. Agnew was a unionist during the Civil War but may have retained some sympathy for southern ways. According to a history of Beaver County, Pennsylvania, Agnew's home, the judge said more than once that, had his family remained in Mississippi, he would have been a rebel. And there were family connections: his first cousin was Varina Howell, wife of Jefferson Davis.

The decision that Agnew read in April 1867 asserted (1) that whites shouldn't be expected to behave decently when in close quarters with blacks, (2) that railroads were within their rights—and were perhaps performing a duty—to segregate and (3) that separate but equal was okay.

"It is not an unreasonable regulation for a common carrier to seat passengers so as to preserve order and decorum," noted the decision. "If a Negro take his seat beside a white man or his wife or daughter, the law cannot repress the anger, or conquer the aversion which some will feel."

WC&PR, noted the decision, had not refused to transport Miles and had not asserted her inferiority. It merely assigned separate seats. "The ladies' car," noted the court by analogy, "is known upon every well-regulated railroad, implies no loss of equal right on the part of the excluded sex and its propriety is doubted by none."

Finally, Agnew's court sympathized with the railroad's need to maintain order, concluding, "It is much wiser to avert the consequences of this repulsion of race by separation, than to punish afterward the breach of the peace it may have caused."

A few months later, the decision became moot when Lowry's bill became law. That law prohibited discrimination and effectively overruled the decision's effect in Pennsylvania. But the decision remained on the books for thirty years until resurrected by another, higher court. (Ironically, three days after Lowry's bill became law, Catto's fiance, Catherine LeCount, was refused entry to a streetcar by a conductor who shouted in her face, "We don't allow niggers to ride." She appealed to a magistrate, who refused to act because he had not yet received official notice of the law. LeCount obtained an official copy of the bill and took it to the magistrate, who then arrested and fined the conductor $100).

In 1892 in Louisiana, a black man named Homer Plessy boarded a "white" car on the East Louisiana Railroad, sat down and refused to leave. He was arrested, jailed and, later, convicted for violating the state segregation law. Plessy's appeals reached the U.S. Supreme Court. In 1896, in *Plessy v. Ferguson*, the court ruled that the separate-but-equal doctrine was constitutional and cited *WC&PR v. Miles* among other cases.

Accommodations were never equal. Under the Jim Crow system blessed by *Plessy*, white and black schools were not funded equally. Black moviegoers got the lousy balcony seats. Public drinking fountains, restrooms and parks were segregated. White motorists had the right of way at intersections.

This way of life continued until 1954 when, in *Brown v. Board of Education*, the U.S. Supreme Court ordered the desegregation of public schools in Little Rock, Arkansas. Ruling that separate was not equal after all, *Brown* finally reversed the *Plessy* decision. And when *Plessy* went, so went the unintended consequences of Mary Miles's refusal to ride home to Hinsonville with the other black folks.

1869

WHAT FOOLS THESE
MORTALS BE!

Today, we have *America's Funniest Home Videos* and reality television for proof that humans aren't too bright. Our ancestors had to rely on the daily papers.

And—truthfully?—editors have always had plenty to work with. People in the 1860s tempted fate in ways no less lamebrained than now. Not long ago, for instance, a popular TV show showed a clip of a man using a power saw to cut the supports of a roof on which he was standing. In March 1869, three Chester County men held down the safety valve on a steam engine just to see what would happen. Here's how the *West Chester Jeffersonian* reported it:

Explosion—The citizens of Unionville in East Marlborough township had a steam boiler explosion last week which, though not on a very large scale, might have resulted more seriously. It appears that Mr. Wilson Loller had built a model engine for his own amusement, the boiler of which was made of tin, holding about a gallon of water, and had it running with a very light pressure of steam. Three young men of the village, named John G. Marshall, Joel Durnal and Jos. Myers, hearing of it, and not being particularly engaged, visited Mr. Loller's place of business, and not liking his supervision or skill as an engineer, concluded to run the "machine" on their approved plan. They at once set to work—Durnall holding down the "safety valve," Marshall performing the part of a pair of bellows, while Myers added "fuel to the flames," when the boiler exploded with a slight report, scalding all three pretty severely.

In 1871, carpenter John Pyle rode the train to Oxford and then decided to walk home on the tracks. Then he decided to take a nap on the tracks. His subsequent death under a Maryland-bound train is one of many examples of our ancestors' failure to think. *Dolores Rowe.*

See the pattern? As in "men" and "dumb"? Our grandfathers did dumb things with locomotives. With horses and dogs. With firearms. With large, sharp, high-powered saws. The means change, but the Y chromosome is a gift that keeps on giving.

Locally, the phenomenon began in prehistory when a young Native American decided to explore a Howellville cave without waiting for the flashlight to be invented. In 1879, some mineralogists emerged from the cave with his jaw, leg and other bones, which they turned over to property owner William W. Jefferis.

"The glenoid cavity of the shoulder bone is quite well preserved," reported the *Local.* "Projecting from it are a number of [stalagmites]." The paper didn't mention the formations' length, but in this climate, stalagmites typically grow about two inches in five hundred years.

Then there was the acrobat wannabe whose story was told by the Pennsburg *Town & Country* in 1904. William Fahringer, sixteen and an apprentice at Miles Saw Mill in West Manayunk, had thought it would be a neat idea to perform acrobatics over a high-speed saw.

"Having a few minutes to spare, Fahringer undertook to show the workmen how to 'skin the cat' on an overhead steam pipe," reported the newspaper. "He stepped lightly unto the sawing table, swung his body over the pipe and just as he came back to poise lost his grip. When the boy's left leg came in contact with the saw, it bit cleanly through the flesh and bone before Fahringer knew he had been hurt. A workman grabbed at the boy to haul him out of danger and got hold of the severed limb, which came away in his grasp. The man uttered a scream, dropped the leg and fainted."

Yesterday's foolishness with firearms might seem quaint. A century ago, there were still lots of muzzleloaders around—the sort of gun loaded by pouring in powder, wadding and, finally, shot that was tamped down with a ramrod. To make a bigger impact, one put in more power and more shot—up to a point.

Like the point exceeded by West Chester attorney Wesley C. Talbot in 1878 when he decided to exterminate some noisy cats on the roof of a building next to his office. According to the *Daily Local News*, "Talbot procured a large pistol and this he gave to Joseph Melton with the instructions to charge it heavily and return it to him. Joseph accordingly repaired to the [dry goods] store of Messrs. Kinnard & Pyle and there put in a profuse quantity of powder and about a handful of large shot, and having done so, returned it."

The cats returned. Talbot picked up his gun. Identifying the leader, he chased it into an adjoining yard and aimed. "Then came a terrific explosion," reported the newspaper, "such as only proceeds from a weapon of terrible death-dealing power. The weapon, unhappily for Mr. Talbot, bursted." Talbot's hand flew up and struck him in the face with what was left of the gun, creating some bloody wounds. But he survived. Oh, and by the way, "He killed the cat," reported the *Local*.

Melvin F. Bitting tried a similar stunt at Limeport on New Year's Eve 1903 when he joined "a number of young men…discharging firearms as [was] an old custom," according to the *T&C*. Bitting was using an old musket, and "in this he loaded some extra heavy charges of powder in order to make a loud report." He survived with most of his hand.

Also in 1903, the *T&C* reported on two Norristown boys who decided to duplicate the Hamilton-Burr duel. Eugene Fulmer and Edward Shinners, both sixteen, "stood back to back and then stepped off three paces. As they turned to fire, the sleeve of Shinner's coat caught in the trigger and the hammer snapped." The ball struck Fulmer in the left eye, which doctors later removed.

How about dumb pet tricks? The story of how Antonio Buiortiro got himself killed in 1904 probably equals—in applied intellect—that of the trash haulers whose runaway truck damaged Swann Fountain in 2004. (The driver got out, put the truck in neutral and didn't put on the brake. Duh.)

Buiortiro got off his horse while riding near Edge Hill in July and allowed the animal to graze. But to keep it from wandering, Buiortiro tied it with a long rope—one end to the horse's halter and one to his ankle.

"A train frightened the horse," reported the *T&C*, and Buiortiro was dragged over a mile across hard road and a railroad crossing. When found, "Buiortiro's head was split open, his body horribly lacerated and his clothes torn from the body."

Two months later, Tony Acario, a worker at a quarry near Pottstown, left a stick of dynamite lying around the property. Acario's goat swallowed the dynamite. In a story headlined "Goat Ate Dynamite and Is Now Alone," the *T&C* reported, "Efforts to capture the animal without using unnecessary force have failed, and the goat has been at liberty for three days, a menace to the safety of the 150 laborers employed at the quarry. It is probable the animal will have to be poisoned."

Even a barn can be deadly. In 1886, while reminiscing about his Civil War–era boyhood in Frazer to the *New York Times*, writer William Drysdale (1852–1901) told of his friend, Jim, who lived along Lancaster Pike on a farm with "a typical Pennsylvania barn, three times as big as the house."

Jim's game was climbing to the peak of the barn's roof—fifty or sixty feet above the ground—and sliding off at high speed to land in a haystack. "But this unaccustomed motion started some of the nails in the shingles, and one mean-spirited little nail worked itself up half an inch or so," recalled Drysdale. "It caught him exactly in that part of his trousers on which he was riding. The trousers and the nail were both solid, and he hung there helpless until his big brother came with a ladder and rescued him."

Jim had bad luck. One Fourth of July, he carried a bottle of gunpowder to school and buried it to make a "volcano." The fuse didn't seem to be working, so Jim put his eye down to the hole to see about it.

"That was the last thing he saw at all for several weeks," said Drysdale. "Some of us led him home, to stay in retirement till his eyebrows grew out again." Years later, when he was trimming a tree, a big limb fell on Jim and killed him.

There also seems to have been a tendency to lie on train tracks, as Jennersville carpenter John Pyle did in March 1871. After riding the train to Oxford to buy tools, Pyle evidently decided to walk home on the tracks of the Philadelphia & Baltimore Central Railroad. After a mile or so, he laid down on the tracks for a nap. About forty-five minutes later, a Maryland-bound train carried him for a few yards on its cowcatcher before he fell under the wheels.

More than thirty years later, two unnamed Italians met an express train while crossing the Schuylkill on a railroad bridge. One laid on a ledge on the side of the bridge and survived without a scratch. The second laid between the rails; the next day, his trouser pocket containing a small sum of money was found on the cowcatcher, his leg on the riverbank and his body in the river.

But for sheer scale of near catastrophe, let's salute the men of Kennett Square who, in the Gettysburg panic of 1863, concluded that rebels were camped in Samuel Thompson's woods southwest of town.

"The appeal to arms was sounded and forty men and boys presented themselves in front of the hall with muskets, shotguns, swords and pistols," the *Kennett Advance* recalled in 1882. As the boys patrolled the streets, the men deployed a skirmish line and moved toward the woods.

"When the immediate vicinity of the rebel camp was reached," the story continued, "'General' John T. Chambers divided his forces into two parties that he might the more completely surround the camp." One group went one way and one group the other. Then, both commands started into the woods.

Eventually, the two groups met and nearly fired volleys at each other. They scoured the woods and then returned to tell the town that no Confederates were near.

Their neighbors, of course, were quite close at hand. A chilling thought indeed.

1869

CARPETBAGGING

Politics is no place for anyone who ever had an original thought. Which leaves us with...well, pretty much what we have.

Take Chester County abolitionist J. Williams Thorne (1816–1897), who moved to North Carolina after the Civil War to farm and—he fervently hoped—help build a new, more democratic South. Thorne even got himself elected to the North Carolina legislature. But his political enemies—including many ex-Confederates hostile to racial equality—pounced on Thorne's unconventional religious views, which they used to expel him from his seat.

"Ostensibly, I was expelled on account of my religious opinions," Thorne wrote to the editor of the *West Chester Republican*, "but really because I was a Radical Republican."

It could have been worse. If Thorne had been African American in that time and place, he might have been lynched.

Born to a Quaker family, Thorne was a thoughtful, serious youth with an early taste for literature. He could recite poetry by the hour—Milton and Robert Burns, in particular. According to family lore, he once walked twenty miles to Wilmington to buy books.

As an adult, Thorne became a strict vegetarian who used the Bible, science and history to prove his the only fit diet for mankind. He kept his dog on a meatless diet and insisted to visitors that the animal had "all the wisdom of Solomon" compared to his neighbors' meat-eating dogs. He didn't push vegetarianism on others, but when a son killed a chicken, Thorne was heard to grumble that "[e]very time someone gets hungry around here, we have to kill something."

Abolitionist J. Williams Thorne of Chester County moved south after the Civil War, thinking that he could help reform it into a more egalitarian society. Elected to the North Carolina legislature, his unorthodox religious beliefs made him vulnerable to criticism from ex-Confederates. *Nancy Plumley.*

Thorne and his wife, Mary Pusey, opposed slavery. But they did not share the then common belief that the best response to slavery was to abstain from participating in the system that supported it. William Lloyd Garrison was famous for dismissing the U.S. Constitution as a "covenant with Hell" that gave legal protection to slavery. Wendell Phillips argued that no true abolitionist would hold office because doing so required an oath of allegiance to that tainted document. Many refused even to vote.

Thorne believed it the duty of reformers to make change happen, by speaking, writing, voting and holding office. He sought opportunities to do them all. Thorne supported the Liberty Party, which proposed to abolish slavery through political action.

Local historian R.C. Smedley reported an 1850 confrontation between Thorne and fellow Quaker Thomas Whitson. Whitson, a nonparticipating Garrisonian abolitionist, was trying to make Thorne see that politics equaled support of slavery.

"Would thee be willing, against the pro-slavery clauses of the Constitution, to assist fugitives in escaping from bondage?" asked Whitson.

"Yes," said Thorne promptly. "There is nothing in the Constitution to prevent it. The very spirit of the preamble commands that I shall do it."

"Thee shall have the opportunity," said Whitson.

"I will be glad of it," Thorne declared.

And so, a pact was formed. Thorne's home became an Underground Railroad station. Thorne and his wife Mary also used their house as a school, and one of their teachers, Esther Kent, later married Smedley.

In 1860, Thorne was among the first to learn that a free black had been kidnapped by the "Gap Gang," a band of thieves and counterfeiters that sidelined in returning runaways to their masters.

"In many instances, this gang went boldly to farms where native free negroes were working," reported the *New York Times* in 1888, "and on pretense of arresting them for some alleged crime, carried them off and they were never heard of again."

Thorne and a U.S. marshal arrived in Baltimore in time to stop the sale of the man who is identified in historical accounts only by his last name, Brown. Brown subsequently identified his kidnappers, who were convicted. In retaliation, one member of the Gap Gang set fire to Thorne's barn, which was destroyed, along with his entire harvest and all of his farming equipment.

Thorne's property was insured. But he was a tenacious sort who missed no opportunity to make life hard for defenders of slavery. He sought out witnesses who identified the arsonist, Francis Wilson, and then pestered his insurance company's lawyer to get a statement from a witness lest the man die before Wilson's trial. Wilson, too, was convicted.

Thorne was known in Chester and Lancaster Counties as a skilled debater and writer. He was a regular at area lyceums, where people listened as speakers dissected the issues of the day. A fellow debater wrote of him: "[Thorne] was an able, clear, forcible and singularly skillful debater, always fair and good humored. When he got his antagonist in a hole, he took care to keep him in it, but he did it so pleasantly that no one could find fault." In 1851, Thorne wrote an account of the Christiana Riot, in which local blacks killed a slave hunter.

"The Christiana Riot and the subsequent conduct of the southerners and their allies," wrote Thorne, "had the effect of opening the eyes of the people of the north to the iniquities of the Fugitive Slave Law and the power it gave the slave hunters to run roughshod over the rights and privileges of the people of the North."

Such activism makes enemies. Possible evidence of this may be seen in the 1860 census, which recorded Thorne and his family as black. The census was taken by a local physician, William S. Latta, who was more conservative than Thorne in nearly everything. Perhaps Latta thought this would be a good joke on a local oddball known to oppose the census practice of classifying people by race.

Locally, Thorne was just another eccentric—and Chester County had many—who amused himself and others with speeches and letters to the editor. He was intelligent and honest but could never have been elected to anything. But after he moved to North Carolina in 1869, he found himself in a very different environment.

Convincing Southerners of their errors had been an abolitionist dream for years. Before the Civil War, according to Chris Densmore, curator of Swarthmore's Friends Historical Library, various utopians talked of planting free-labor communities in the upper South to demonstrate "that free labor was more economically efficient than slave labor."

But almost no one actually went. Among Thorne's fellow Quakers at Longwood Meeting near Kennett Square, only Thorne moved south. Surprisingly, for one so outspoken, he seems to have left no clear statement as to why he went. He may have been motivated by idealism, economic opportunity or both.

In any case, the Thornes sold their Chester County house, bought 1,700 acres in Warren County, northeast of Raleigh, and commenced raising cotton and apples.

When Thorne arrived, Congress had recently rejected President Andrew Johnson's mild form of Reconstruction for a tougher version emphasizing racial equality. Radical Republicans pushed through the Fourteenth Amendment defining citizenship and guaranteeing equal protection to all. Former Confederate states were required to ratify the amendment and write new constitutions that reflected its principles.

In North Carolina—where voting rights had previously been restricted to male taxpayers—the new 1868 constitution abolishing property qualifications was supported by many whites. Working with freed slaves, they created the North Carolina Republican Party, which elected a governor and a majority of the legislature in the 1868 elections. Opposing them were the Democrats, unreconstructed ex-Confederates and upper-class whites who had lost their monopoly on power.

Thorne, of course, was a Republican. And because he was educated, articulate and fully in sympathy with the new world order, Thorne seemed like a good candidate. He spoke widely to condemn Democrats' efforts to create separate black and white schools, in defiance of the new constitution's requirement for a "general and uniform system." Democrats responded by ridiculing his appearances on the same platforms as African Americans, part of their long-term (and ultimately successful) strategy to separate blacks and poor whites. In 1874, Thorne ran for Warren County's seat in the state House of Representatives and won.

Then Thorne's habit of speaking his mind worked against him.

Soon after the election, Democrats seized on a pamphlet that Thorne had written several years earlier debunking evangelical Christianity. In particular, Thorne attacked the idea that one must be a conservative, Bible-based Christian to be moral.

"The evangelical church has almost always defended a popular wrong and opposed an unpopular right," wrote Thorne. "This course is reversed by the unbelieving infidel or liberal." Conservative Christians, he insisted, had defended slavery and were now the worst racists. He also dismissed the importance of the Sabbath.

Such thoughts were common enough among freethinkers but never politically popular. A resolution was introduced declaring Thorne's writings "subversive of good government and morals" that "render him unqualified to render the duties of a legislator."

The House ignored affidavits from ministers that Thorne was no atheist. But it did give him an hour to defend himself—an hour during which Thorne blistered the body's members.

"He showed that he not only believed in a God, but in a great deal better God than they worshipped," wrote R.J. Houston of Lancaster in an 1897 tribute to Thorne, "a God who did not sanction drunkenness or gambling or fighting, as he presumed their God did, since nearly all of them engaged in these things; a God who would sometime mete out justice to the Ku Klux Klan, then murdering innocent people all over the state, which they seemed to encourage."

He changed no minds and was expelled. But Thorne returned to the capitol in 1876 as a senator. Over time, though, the balance of power slipped to the Democrats, partly due to the parliamentary skill demonstrated in this episode and partly due to physical intimidation that suppressed Republican political power. The result was the South's Jim Crow system, which lasted until the 1960s.

Thorne had a better vision, of course, but that was his undoing.

1874

ART GUIDED BY SCIENCE

You're a juror in a death penalty case. The primary piece of evidence is a photograph. Is that enough to sentence a man to death?

Increasingly, it isn't. Photoshop and other photo-manipulation software have eroded trust in what we see. Courts now have elaborate procedures to prove that images have not been doctored. Standard rules of evidence, for instance, require prosecutors to preserve digital images in their original formats and to save copies as read-only files.

It's a trend 136 years too late for William Udderzook, who went to the hangman in West Chester in 1874. Udderzook had been convicted of stabbing to death a man whose identity was proved by a photograph that no one—other than a desperate defense attorney—challenged. The case was a landmark in confirming the legal admissibility of photographs in court.

"The process [of photography] is one in general use so common we cannot refuse to take judicial cognizance of it as a proper means of producing a correct likeness," wrote Daniel Agnew, chief justice of the Pennsylvania Supreme Court, in rejecting Udderzook's appeal. "It is a result of art guided by certain principles of science."

It began as insurance fraud. William Eachus Udderzook and Winfield Scott Goss both lived in Baltimore, had married sisters and knew each other well. Udderzook worked for a sawmill. Goss, a self-employed maker and gilder of picture frames, had a small workshop located on the outskirts of the city. On the side, according to Philadelphia journalist Louis Megargee, Goss was trying to invent a substitute for tree rubber, using ingredients that he kept in the shop.

Murdered near Atglen in 1872, Winfield Scott Goss was later identified with the aid of a photograph. It was one of the first times that a photograph was used as evidence in a capital case. *Chester County Historical Society.*

Perhaps picture frames weren't selling. Perhaps Goss was frustrated by his unsuccessful experiments. Perhaps Udderzook hated his dirty job at the mill. Perhaps all of it. In any case, Goss had $25,000 worth of life insurance from four different companies. In February 1872, he acted with Udderzook on a scheme to collect the money without undergoing the inconvenience of dying.

The fire that leveled Goss's workshop was blamed on a defective lamp. An inquest revealed that Goss had just bought a gallon of kerosene for the one-quart fixture. Goss's chemicals also fed the flames.

"The body of a man was seen in the glowing embers," wrote Megargee. "Hooks were procured and the corpse, black and bleeding, was drawn from the ruins." The face was burned beyond recognition. The legs and arms were nearly burned off. But the body was roughly Goss's size, and a tuft of unburned hair was the color of his. A coroner ruled that the body was Goss's and that he had died by fire from an accidental explosion. Case closed. The body was turned over to Goss's family, viewed by many (strong-stomached) friends and relatives—none of whom suspected anything amiss—and buried.

The insurers were suspicious. Three of the four policies had been purchased within the past ten months. Goss had closed a bank account the day before the fire. Goss's brother, Campbell, claimed that he was at home the night of the fire, although his landlord and two members of his family all testified that he was not. (The insurers were sure that Campbell Goss was aiding his brother's getaway.)

Is photography reliable? Skeptics can point to tricks like this composite image by a nineteenth-century photographer, who seems to be photographing himself. Convicted killer William Udderzook tried to debunk photographic evidence on such grounds but went to the gallows anyway. *Library of Congress.*

Campbell Goss denied having rented a horse and buggy on the night of the fire, although he was positively identified by the livery owner. (The insurers suspected that he had driven his brother to the train station.) Later, Campbell Goss visited the scene of the fire and "discovered" Goss's watch and keys—missed by everyone else. (The insurers suspected that he had planted them.) Goss's widow testified that her husband had good teeth, yet an examination of the exhumed corpse revealed that many of its teeth were decayed or missing.

Udderzook's testimony was that of someone who "knew too much," according to investigators John B. Lewis, MD, and Charles C. Bombaugh, MD. He had spent several hours in the late afternoon with Goss. "He had visited every room in the cottage…and knew there was no one in the house except himself and Goss," wrote Lewis and Bombaugh. "He also knew there was no dead body in the house." And Udderzook just happened to have left the building fifteen or so minutes before the fire erupted.

Investigators also thought it odd that Goss, who was strong and healthy, did not at least try to flee the burning building.

The Mutual, Continental, Travelers and Knickerbocker insurance companies all refused to pay. Goss's wife sued and won, though the suit took nearly eighteen months. Then, in July 1873, as the insurers were vowing an appeal, a strange story filtered down from Chester County. Another body had been found near Penningtonville (now Atglen), and Udderzook had been seen acting strangely in the vicinity.

Investigators soon focused on a man calling himself A.C. Wilson who had checked into a boardinghouse near Bryn Mawr in June 1872, four months after the fire. Wilson stayed until November and then moved to other boardinghouses nearby. Early on June 27, Wilson checked out of a Philadelphia hotel, announcing that he was heading for a train that would carry him to New York and an afternoon steamer for Europe. What followed remains unknown, but Wilson was seen with Udderzook on June 30 at the West Grove railroad station. Both checked into a tavern in Jennersville and spent the night.

"The next morning," Megargee later wrote, "Udderzook left his companion, who appeared to be drinking heavily and ill and rode to the house of his sister, Mrs. Samuel Rhoades, living near [Atglen], about 13 miles away." Samuel Rhoades later testified that Udderzook had offered him $1,000 to help drug and rob a man. The man, said Udderzook, had developed delirium tremens, was drinking his money away and probably wouldn't live long anyway. Rhoades refused.

Udderzook then rented a horse and buggy, in which he and Wilson drove north from Jennersville at about 6:30 p.m. on July 1. Udderzook arrived, alone, at Atglen at 11:40 p.m. and returned the vehicle, battered and stained with blood. Wilson was never seen alive again.

Ten days later, on July 11, Gainer Moore, a local resident, noticed a large number of buzzards as he was passing Baer's Woods, a mile or so from Atglen. The buzzards were on the fence, perched in the bushes and in trees and walking around in the road. He investigated and found a partially buried human torso, which had been stabbed eight or nine times. The severed legs and one arm were buried nearby.

"At the time…I raised the head out from the ground, the face had a natural look," Moore later testified. "By that, I mean I could have recognized it easily if I had known the person in life."

Initial press coverage drew the attention of the insurance companies resisting the Widow Goss's claims. They sent a physician with Goss's photograph to examine the corpse. Observers all agreed that the photo resembled the body on the table. And the physician confirmed that the body had excellent teeth.

To investigators, it was now clear. Udderzook and Goss had conspired to defraud the insurance companies, and Goss—bored and restless after months in hiding—had become a liability. Udderzook killed Goss to prevent his own role from being revealed. But how to prove this in court?

There was much circumstantial evidence. Witnesses had seen Udderzook and this "Wilson" together. There was Udderzook's documented testimony in the insurance case. But the prosecution's case rested on proving that Goss and Wilson were the same man. To that end, the key piece of evidence was Goss's photograph, which was shown to Moore on the witness stand.

"This person bears a strong resemblance to the face of the person I discovered in Baer's Woods," said Moore. "From the point of the nose upwards, in particular, there is a strong resemblance; also in the eyebrows and the hair." Moore testified that he had "immediately" recognized the man without prompting from prosecutor W.M. Hayes. Udderzook was convicted and condemned.

The use of photography by the criminal justice system was not entirely new. In 1859, the U.S. Supreme court had noted the usefulness of "the beautiful art of photography" in grouping together on a single sheet for examination a collection of genuine and disputed signatures. In the 1860s, a "rogues gallery" of wanted criminals was common in urban police departments. In France, Emperor Napoleon III (1808–1873) had fantasized while rebuilding Paris about "photographic batteries, so located as to take, from many points of view at once, the likenesses of persons engaged in disturbing the peace."

But as photography's presence in daily life expanded, lawyers debated its legal status. Some saw photography as similar to hearsay, a he said/she said equivalent. In 1869, a writer for the *American Law Register* sought to debunk this view: "Human memory will fade…and can be distorted or intentionally falsified. But the photograph 'is that person himself, precisely as he exists in the article of vision—is, therefore, direct and original evidence of the kind of man he was.'"

In his appeal, Udderzook's lawyer rejected this view. The only acceptable proof, insisted J. Perdue, was testimony by someone who had known Goss and who had also inspected the body of Wilson. A photograph was merely a copy of the negative, which in turn was only a copy of the subject—two times removed from reality and, therefore, unreliable.

Bunk, said Agnew.

On November 12 at 12:19 p.m., after shaking Udderzook's hand, Chester County sheriff Davis Gill threw the lever on the scaffold. "Death ensued by strangulation," reported the *New York Times*, "with apparent suffering."

Photoshop *that*.

1881

SCHMOOZING THE LADIES

Befriending the customer is a key principle of modern marketing. And if the customer is a woman, one easy way to befriend her is to show that you share her cherished beliefs—including the belief that men are hopeless shoppers.

"Women take pride in their ability to shop prudently and well," writes retail guru Paco Underhill—a pride based, in part, on the conviction that men don't do it as well.

In fact, this sort of pandering has been around a long time. More than a century ago, Philip M. Sharples (1857–1944), founder of the Sharples Cream Separator Company of West Chester, made high art of flattering and winning female customers. In response, women made Sharples the top-selling device for separating cream from milk. Together, Sharples and his customers turned the nickel-and-dime business of farm dairying into an industry that generated serious folding money.

First, though, a word about milk, which has only been an "industry" since about 1830. In the colonial era, cattle were valued mostly for their meat, hides and ability to pull a wagon or plow. Milk was a relatively minor byproduct because cattle simply didn't eat well enough to produce much of it. In 1759, according to Wilmington minister Israel Acrelius, cows produced about four quarts of milk per day "when the pasture is fair." (Today, the average U.S. dairy cow produces more than twenty-two quarts per day.) After 1800, production gradually increased with better feeding and breeding.

But there were also habits to change. Early Americans didn't drink milk. Mostly, they processed the cream into butter and cheese and then mixed the remaining "skim" milk with grain and fed it to pigs or calves. Excess butter and cheese were sold, but there simply wasn't enough of it to produce much income.

Separating cream was also tedious and time-consuming. Until the mid-nineteenth century, fresh milk was poured into heavy earthenware crocks and then placed in the cold (fifty-four to fifty-six degrees) water of a springhouse. Eventually, the cream rose to the top and was ladled off by hand.

By tradition, dairying was considered women's work. ("Daierie" is Old English for "servant girl.") As late as 1901, according to a Pennsylvania Department of Agriculture report, the state's typical German

FARM PLEASURES

Men were good for brute labor in Sharples Cream Separator advertising but little else. The company was a pioneer in marketing to a mostly female audience. *Chester County Historical Society.*

farmer maintained "a terrible aversion to milking a cow. He looks upon it as a disgrace to his manhood, and all the milking done in this section of Pennsylvania [York and adjacent counties] for many years was done by the female portion of the family."

In 1878, a Swedish engineer named Gustaf de Laval introduced the first continuous separator to use centrifugal force to separate a liquid's heavier and lighter elements. It was first used in Norway to separate fish oil. In 1881, Sharples, who owned a small West Chester machine shop, talked De Laval into granting him a distributorship in Chester County. A few years later, P.M., as he was known, was licensed to manufacture De Laval's machines for the U.S. market.

Then P.M. got really ambitious. He "made…improvements" to De Laval's design that, he said, made "the cream flow more easily, making smoother cream and saving considerable power." P.M. secured a patent and began to manufacture his own line of separators. De Laval sued for patent infringement.

"We had a great time, with 17 or 18 patent suits," P.M. told the *West Chester Local* newspaper in 1931. "However, I beat them to a finish and was ready to go ahead. I made my own designs, and instead of paying a royalty to them, they were paying it to me."

The Sharples cream separator was a huge success. At its height at the turn of the twentieth century, the company employed several hundred men at its Patton Avenue plant, producing up to sixty thousand separators annually. Eventually, Sharples also opened factories in Chicago, San Francisco, Toronto and Hamburg, Germany. In 1911, the company bought a West Virginia coal mine to ensure a steady supply of fuel.

This sort of success automatically makes a man a leading citizen. So, in addition to running his own company, P.M. was a founder of the Pennsylvania Parks Association, vice-president of the Keystone Automobile Club and a member of the board of managers at Swarthmore College. He and his wife, Helen, lived on the north side of West Chester in an immense mansion called Greystone, whose private lake they opened to the public for swimming during the summer.

The Sharples separator was not the only such device on the market and may or may not have been the best. But the company excelled in talking to farm women in a way that both addressed their concerns and helped them define what those concerns should be—profit, convenience and long-term reliability.

In 1908, for instance, U.S. agricultural publications carried a Sharples ad comparing its "Tubular" separator to four competing machines. Standing among all the hardware was an average-sized, average-looking woman with her hand resting lightly on the Sharples machine. The text went on to explain how the woman reached her thoroughly considered decision.

"The young woman beside [the Sharples machine] is only five feet four inches tall," noted the ad. "Yet the Tubular's supply can is hardly as high as her waist [and] the crank is set just right for easy turning." It was all about convenience. Competing machines, noted the company, required operators to lift full buckets of milk to head height. They also set their cranks low, so operators had to bend over as they cranked.

In truth, there were other machines with low supply tanks and convenient cranks. But none matched Sharples's adeptness at selling the idea that its machine would spare the owner an aching back.

Hand-cranked cream separators were marketed to many farm women. But centralized dairying and the Great Depression made farm-based operations and separators—like this one at a 1930s farm auction—obsolete. *Library of Congress.*

This fact-oriented theme pervaded all Sharples marketing, to a degree that might seem counterproductive. Among the company's publications was *Business Dairying*, which explained in excruciating detail the superiority of its inner workings: "The law of centrifugal force is that it increases as the square of the number of revolutions, but decreases directly as the diameter [of the bowl] increases."

The publication also detailed the concept of "nutritive ratio"—basically, that cattle feed should contain one part protein to six parts carbohydrates and fats. There are many ways to produce such feed, but Sharples's message was that farmers could save money by including skim milk produced by its separator. According to a chart, ten pounds of corn fodder, ten pounds of mixed hay and eight pounds of wheat bran, when mixed with twenty pounds of skim milk, would produce feed with a protein to carb/fat nutritive ratio of 1:5.4.

Got all that? It's likely that many of Sharples's customers didn't quite grasp it either, but that's not really the point. When marketing to women, says Underhill, a key principle is to appeal to their sense of themselves as smart shoppers. For women, gathering information is an essential part of shopping, so a wise merchant comes prepared with lots of it. (Men likely never read the Sharples brochure.)

It worked. Sharples advertising brimmed with testimonials. In 1908, Dora Kitely of Wilmot, Michigan, wrote: "We have gained one-quarter as much again [in cream volume] by using the Tubular. We have saved one-half of the work. We have succeeded finely in feeding young stock with Tubular-separated milk. Everyone around here thinks the Tubular is the best. We cannot recommend our separator too highly, and we would not be without it for twice the price." From Ballwin, Missouri, Hilkea Bopp boasted that "we gained seven pounds of butter the first week after giving up the [competing separator] that we had used for 10 years."

Men were useful as illustrations of foolishness. In an ad that ran before World War I, Sharples described an (unnamed) farmer's experience with a separator whose forty-five parts had to be hand-washed twice a day. The Sharples machine, in contrast, had just eleven such parts. "He saw the [parts] before he bought the machine, but he did not appreciate what thoroughly washing them twice a day meant," explained the company. Could anyone but a man be so clueless?

Another theme was man-as-beast-of-burden. In most Sharples ads, it is a woman who selects and operates a separator; men tote the milk pails.

For a few decades, women ruled a profitable and growing industry. Technology allowed them to expand production. Meanwhile, urbanization meant that fewer people owned cows, so the market for fluid milk also expanded—made possible by better transportation. But the era began to fade in the early twentieth century. Trucking milk to centralized dairy operations offered economies of scale that farm operations couldn't match. Then the Great Depression wiped out most remaining farm dairies. Sharples declared bankruptcy in 1933; today, the company's patents are owned by Gustaf de Laval's old company, Alfa Laval.

But some things never change. In the first decade of the twenty-first century, TurboTax debuted a TV ad in which the hubby repeatedly scratches his head over the software even as his wife cashes the refund check. Advertising's clueless male lives on.

1886

THE RISE OF THE CLERKS

Asking nicely gets you nowhere. Boiled down, this is why we have unions and big government.

This brings us to retail clerks and their crummy hours. (Crummy [kruhm-ee], *adj*. Weekends, holidays, night shifts, Black Fridays.) In retail, such hours come with the territory. And it used to be worse. In 1888, the average U.S. retail employee earned ten dollars per week for eighty-six hours of work while receiving no holidays, no sick pay, no pensions and no insurance. Stores commonly opened at 8:00 a.m. and closed at 10:00 p.m. There were no shifts. Clerks worked fourteen hours a day, six days a week.

But in 1886, West Chester clerks led by James McCabe, Howard Wilson and George Taylor tried asking employers to voluntarily reduce daily hours to twelve: 8:00 a.m. to 8:00 p.m. Despite some temporary successes, the international "early closing movement" failed here just as it did everywhere else.

"We would do more work, have lighter hearts and be better generally by closing at 8 than at 9 or 10 o'clock," one clerk told the *Daily Local News*. Shorter hours would allow clerks to attend religious and cultural events, advance themselves through study and participate in democracy, as well as—not insignificantly—go courting.

The flaw? The movement was voluntary. No laws regulated retail hours. Store owners were free to participate or not. Many employers were willing to cooperate, but on the condition that all other stores close, too. But there always seemed to be one who refused. Then it was late hours again for everyone.

Clerks at Darlington Grocery and elsewhere organized in the 1880s to convince West Chester store owners to voluntarily reduce hours to twelve per day. Some retailers went along, but there was always a holdout, so the movement failed. *Chester County Historical Society.*

"Ultimately, early closing highlighted the impracticability of [the voluntary] approach," wrote Australian historians Michael Quinlan, Margaret Gardner and Peter Akers in a study of the movement there. "Divisions between small and large shopkeepers, regional variations, customer preferences, limited organization and solidarity amongst shop employees (and the cheapness of shop labor) and the capacity of a few financially marginal or greedy shop owners to fracture any agreement fatally weakened the movement."

Work hours became an issue during the Industrial Revolution, when manufacturing moved from homes—where workers labored alone and set their own hours—to factories staffed by employees who all began and ended work at the same time. Most factories followed the precedent set by farmers "to begin as soon in the morning and work as late at night as they could see," wrote historian Henry Graham Ashmead.

"It was only as it progressed, and the numbers engaged therein increased, and the necessity of all being employed at one time for the general good, that it became monotonous," he continued. By the mid-nineteenth century, wrote Ashmead, the monotony of factory work was thought worse than the treadmills that British prison inmates were forced to walk for hours.

In Britain, factory hours were first restricted in 1847, with a ten-hour limit for women and children. Men's hours weren't restricted in Britain until 1874. About the same time, labor organizers began agitating the issue in Philadelphia, Manayunk and Delaware County, where Nether Providence millworkers were the core of the movement.

At a December 1847 meeting at Hinkson's Corner, workers resolved that long hours were "particularly injurious to children employed in factories, depriving them in a majority of cases from ever acquiring the rudiments of a common education" and to women by "depriving them of the opportunity of acquiring the necessary knowledge of domestic duties to enable them to fill their stations in well-regulated households." Newspapers also lent support.

"Let those who oppose it just drop into a factory and work among the dirt and grease for 14 hours each day for a twelvemonth," reported the *Delaware County Republican*, "and tell us at the expiration of that time their opinion of the matter."

Bowing to a public groundswell, the legislature limited cotton, wool, flax, paper and glass factory workers to ten hours per day in 1848. Mill interests called it socialism, and restrictions on child labor, in particular, were widely ignored.

As demands for shorter working hours rose, respect for the traditional day of rest—the Sabbath—ebbed. In the early nineteenth century, Pennsylvania was a place where young boys could be imprisoned for playing ball in the street on Sunday. But modern life seemed increasingly at war with devout sensitivities. The state found itself crisscrossed with canals and railroads that operated on Sundays. And workers who had been confined in factories Monday through Saturday disliked being similarly restricted on Sunday.

Retail clerks were harder to organize than factory workers. So, early closing efforts lagged behind the factory movement by several years. In the 1850s, the movement was still novel enough that Charles Dickens could safely satirize it in his 1853 *Frauds on the Fairies*, a satirical version of the Cinderella story that mocked political correctness.

Describing the efforts of Cinderella's fairy godmother to equip her with a coach and six that would take her to the ball but not abuse its workers, Dickens wrote, she looked "behind a watering-pot for six lizards, which she changed into six footmen, each with a petition in his hand ready to present to the Prince, signed by 50,000 persons, in favor of the early closing movement."

On the East Coast of the United States, the movement peaked in the 1880s. (Sacramento, California clerks didn't organize for this purpose until 1891.) In 1883, *Banker's* magazine reported that it was common to find towns in which 90 percent of businesses were closed on Saturday afternoons. "The tradesman," explained the magazine, "wishes to have an opportunity for recreation and amusement which the hours of his business prohibit him enjoying on the ordinary days of the week."

Baseball historian Jeffrey Keitel credited the early closing movement for spiking attendance at late nineteenth-century games.

In June 1886, Philadelphia dry goods retailer Darlington, Runk & Company challenged competitors to join its plan to close at 5:00 p.m. Monday through Friday and at 1:00 p.m. on Saturday during the summer. "In no city should this movement meet with a more hearty response than in Philadelphia, where so large a proportion of the employees in our large dry-goods establishments are females, who justly earn, by their conscientious devotion to their employers' interest, every consideration," wrote a store representative to *Arthur's Home* magazine. "If half a dozen of our dry-goods merchants will unite on this question, the work is accomplished."

The movement appeared in West Chester in October 1886 when the *Daily Local News* reported that eighty of eighty-four store owners approached had signed a petition in favor of closing at 8:00 p.m. Opponents, noted the paper, insisted that they depended on business from farmers who could not get into town and finish their shopping by that hour.

Proponents, reported the *Local*, "argue that nine cases out of every ten the farmer and his family retire before 8 o'clock and by 8:30 are fast asleep in a feather bed, with plenty of good warm blankets and quilts to cover them, while the clerk and the storekeeper plods on in their weary way, wasting coal oil or gas or electricity, dozing now and then, waiting for the farmer."

An unnamed West Chester grocer, meanwhile, called early closing a no-brainer. Customers would get used to it, he said, and retailers would discover that they had lost no business.

"It's just like delivering orders," the grocer told a newspaper reporter. "A year ago, I made up my mind that I would deliver no orders after 6 o'clock. My customers were a little nettled at the time, but soon got over it, and today they don't think of asking me to have 'it sent down' after that hour."

Meanwhile, other county towns were going along. Phoenixville pharmacists agreed in January 1887 to close for part of Sundays so the staff could attend church. In Coatesville, the *Local* reported jokingly about the man who rushed into the business district after 6:00 p.m. and found himself unable to buy a watermelon.

In West Chester, McCabe, Wilson and Taylor headed a nine-man committee tasked with bringing recalcitrant retailers aboard. Who were those clerks? Such people don't leave many historical tracks.

McCabe may have been the James J. McCabe who, in 1913, committed suicide in Fairmount Park. The *Daily Local News* reported that McCabe had been a clerk for Darlington Brothers grocery store of West Chester, a hotel clerk, a shipyard worker and, briefly, a Philadelphia police officer. According to the newspaper, McCabe was unemployed and despondent.

A Howard Wilson died in West Chester in 1948 at the age of ninety. His obituary described Wilson as a retired carpenter who had been employed by the Sharples Separator Works.

There was no other mention of Taylor at the Chester County Historical Society.

Through the first week of November, the committee met and met again. Then, on November 3, it threw in the towel. "I guess we won't succeed," one clerk told the *Local*. "There are too many kickers. Coatesville is a better and more modern place than this. I guess I'll move up there."

It wasn't a complete failure. Grocers Frank Darlington and A.M. Eachus announced that they would close at 8:00 p.m. regardless of what other stores did. Most, however, went back to their regular late hours.

The issue ebbed and flowed for decades. In 1907, progressive grocer Howard E. Simmons of Downingtown—where early closing agreements had repeatedly collapsed—wrote vociferous letters to the editor endorsing the idea. "If I were one the clerks," said Simmons, "I would move for a union and positively would refuse to work more than 10 hours per day."

Unions were next and then government. The Retail Clerks National Protective Union, chartered in 1890, fought for decades for shorter working hours despite the stain left on the movement by the 1886 Haymarket bombing at a Chicago eight-hour-day rally. Washington ended the argument in 1938 with the Fair Labor Standards Act.

Those holdout retailers should have listened when they were asked nicely.

1889

The Value of Play

Never underestimate a goof-off. For Samuel Leeds Allen (1841–1918), the love of play—a talent he perfected at Westtown School—made him a rich man. It also gave generations of American children something to play *with*.

In 1889, Allen patented the Flexible Flyer, the first steerable snow sled. The Flyer eclipsed memories of Allen's nearly three hundred other inventions, including a fertilizer that resembled the planet Saturn. But Allen, who maintained a lifelong love of play, was not the sort to complain.

"The development in coasters is somewhat typical of that in many other directions," Allen wrote in a short 1896 history of sledding that sought to impress his sober business peers by placing the Flyer squarely in the vanguard of rising U.S. technology. "In nearly all the industries of life, we find an increasing demand for better speed, reduced friction, smoother ways, neater guiding and more accurate advancement." And, oh yes, more fun.

Born in Philadelphia, Allen was the son of a pharmacist. His Quaker father, John, had been a partner in a cracker-baking company but sold out at the outset of the Civil War rather than make hardtack biscuits for the military. Allen was named for his maternal grandfather, Samuel Leeds of Leeds Point, New Jersey.

From his earliest days, Allen preferred mischief, exploration and tinkering to any assigned task. As a boy, he spent summers on an uncle's farm, where he teased the maid by removing the pin from the pump handle. At Westtown—where his father sent him in 1850 to "get him out of the city"—Allen invented a small spring gun that he attached to the underside

Children on Flexible Flyer snow sleds—like these in New York's Central Park in 1914—are the legacy of a Westtown School graduate who tested the design at his alma mater, where it replaced larger, faster and nearly uncontrollable bobsleds. *Library of Congress.*

of his seat. The device had such a hair trigger that anyone walking past would set it off. It earned Allen several swats.

According to his cousin, George B. Allen, also a Westtown student, Allen's nickname was "Skiance"—in part because he was tall and always seemed to be looking at the sky. But the name was also a metaphor for a youngster who often seemed to have his head in the clouds.

Allen was fascinated by anything technically difficult. For fun, he would use a penny to draw a perfect circle and then write the entire Lord's Prayer within it. He could kick a ball farther than any other boy, said George Allen, because he had studied the physics of the problem and "kicked it scientifically."

Naturally, he made his teachers impatient.

"I believe I can't study lessons like other boys, and the teacher says I'm lazy," Allen told his cousin.

"No, thee isn't lazy," George Allen replied. "If thee would just stop inventing all those queer things that run across the desk, thee could study as well as anyone else. It is *not* that thee *can't*, but thee *don't*."

Shenanigans aside, Allen was not a bad kid. Among his earliest papers was a list of habits that the young man aimed to acquire or improve: "doing things systematically…finishing everything undertaken…learning something from everyone…politeness, cheerfulness…daily prayer…self-control." And there were some to avoid: temptation; light reading, "which enfeebles the mind and corrupts the heart"; levity on sacred subjects; and cursing.

Eventually, the value of Allen's skills of observation and technology emerged. When he was fourteen, he spent a summer at George Allen's farm in Marple, where his job was helping an employee load hay wagons. Proper loading was essential lest the hay slip off on its way to the barn. Allen watched the man load one wagon.

"After that, Samuel loaded every load of hay and wheat that we hauled that summer," wrote George Allen. "Not one slipped."

After Westtown, Allen attended Friends Select School. He graduated in 1860 and then took over a farm that his father owned near Westfield, New Jersey. Allen was so determined to succeed that he sold his beloved ice skates because he presumed that he wouldn't have time to use them.

"Later he found that farmers did have a little spare time, so he designed a pair that the village blacksmith made," wrote George Allen.

But Allen continued to tinker. In his obituary, the *Philadelphia Evening Telegraph* newspaper described how Allen invented a planter-fertilizer by attaching two tin wash basins together with a metal band. He drilled the band with holes and then mounted the device between two handles. The contraption could be filled with seed or fertilizer and walked over a field like a wheelbarrow.

"Neighboring farmers recognized its value and wished him to make similar implements for them," reported the paper. Because the wash basin fertilizer resembled the planet Saturn with its rings, Allen dubbed it the "Planet Junior" and founded his own firm, the S.L. Allen Company, to produce it and other garden implements. Allen's products, which included drills, cultivators and more, were eventually marketed internationally in a line collectively referred to as "Planets."

Allen was a big success. He became a trustee of Haverford College, of Friends Hospital and, of course, of Westtown. Successful businessmen are always welcome on boards. He was generous philanthropically and with his employees. According to the *Telegraph*, he was among the earliest employers to offer workers life insurance at affordable rates.

Yet Allen maintained his enthusiasm for play. When he took up bicycling, he lobbied his neighbors to build miles of bike paths around their part of New Jersey. When he took up fly-fishing, Allen made his own rods and tied his own flies. (In season, he slept streamside on work nights, woke early, fished until breakfast and then went to the office.) After taking up golf at the age of sixty, Allen won a string of trophies.

"Whatever he went into," said the *Telegraph*, "he did it with such intensity and keenness that not only did he master the sport but became an authority on everything connected with it."

He approached sledding in the same way.

Snow "coasting" appeared early at Westtown (founded 1799), but the students used bobsleds—great heavy contraptions, solidly built, with steel or wooden runners and high in front. Ten or more children could be crowded onto sleds that bore names such as Black Hawk, Mountain Maid and Pride of the Hill. Boys and girls did not ride together, but on the challenging runs two boys were chosen to serve as steersman and surger for the girls.

"The steersman has a difficult task," wrote Westtown historian Helen Hole in 1942. "There is no steering gear [so] with his own feet he must, by judicious kicks at the front runners at just the right moment, direct the thundering mass of nearly a ton into the right path in order to avoid destruction, and yet not reduce speed and so spoil the record of the sled." The job of the surger, who sat at the rear, was to help the bobsled over bumps in the trail by standing at the right moment and then dropping back into his seat, thereby lifting the nose.

"The old letters speak repeatedly of the skill and effectiveness of the surgers," wrote Hole.

Tracks were made by packing down and watering snowy trails through the woods and then waiting overnight as they froze.

Sledding's popularity fell after 1865, when a skating pond was built at Westtown. Then the sport almost disappeared when the stored bobsleds were all destroyed in an 1868 fire. But new sleds were built that were fast and steerable. By the 1880s, sledding was bigger than ever.

Safe? Not entirely. In 1892, one boy received a serious head injury when the bobsled he was riding struck a wagon parked along the trail. No drastic action was taken. Quakers don't ban things. However, wrote Hole, "it became evident that it would be advisable to substitute less dangerous forms of coasting."

Happily, it already existed.

The story most often told is that, in the 1880s, Allen—whose agricultural products were made in the spring and summer—was seeking an off-season product to avoid laying off employees. According to one account, he browsed a dictionary until he came across the word "sled."

Allen experimented with several versions. The Fairy Coaster had steel runners and plush seats and folded for transport but cost fifty dollars. Too expensive. The Fleetwing, given to the Westtown girls in 1884 to try, carried six, was light and had a gong. The Ariel was a hinged bobsled whose front and rear sections steered independently. Hard to control, it crashed so frequently that Westtown boys spoke of Ariel's preference for "climbing trees."

The Flexible Flyer's patent application cited its slated seat and T-shaped runners. Both were new features. But what most distinguished the Flyer was that, by pushing the crossbar to the right or left, the rider could bend the runners and thereby steer the sled. No competitor offered this.

Flyer advertising didn't say so, but the sled was also slower—and therefore safer—than the thundering, two-thousand-pound loaded bobsleds. Plus, if a crash was imminent, riders could simply roll off. Escape was much harder on a bobsled carrying as many as a dozen tightly packed riders.

Still, success was not immediate. Westtown students liked the Flyer, but for years all revenue was consumed by advertising. Finally, about the turn of the twentieth century, Allen gambled that the surging popularity of other outdoor sports—tennis, skating and tobogganing—might carry the Flyer. He convinced Macy's and Wanamaker's department stores to carry the sleds and invested heavily in advertising.

By 1915, Allen could write, "We are sending whole carloads of about 1,200 each to New York, New Haven and Pittsburgh by express; perhaps five full cars in all. There seems little doubt but that we will sell out clean, in all about 120,000."

At Westtown, bobsleds were mostly extinct by 1907. Later students remembered only their Flyers. "Many a Flyer deposited its occupants in a snowdrift," wrote Hole. "The speed still seemed terrific and there was no dearth of excitement and thrills."

Which, of course, was the point.

1914

CREATING EDEN

Fox hunting isn't really about the fox. It's about who rides the horses and who gets ridden over.

This brings us to W. Plunket Stewart (1878–1948), the Baltimore-born securities broker most responsible for creating Philadelphia's "hunt country"—those rolling green miles in southern Chester County.

Before Stewart arrived here in the early twentieth century, the area around Unionville was dominated by working farms of fifty to one hundred acres. By the morning his valet found him dead in bed, Stewart had taken over dozens of farms—more than two thousand acres in all—and removed their fencing to make a playground for himself and his fox hunting friends.

Stewart was born to privilege. His grandfather, David Stewart, founded the Bank of Baltimore, and his father was a wealthy coffee merchant. One of seventeen children, Plunket Stewart attended the Gilman School and then graduated in 1898 from Johns Hopkins University, where his father was a director.

Stewart's first marriage was to Elsie, daughter of A.J. Cassatt, president of the Pennsylvania Railroad. In 1906, the couple moved to Haverford, and Stewart was made a partner in the Philadelphia banking firm of Cassatt & Company. The marriage didn't last, but Stewart seems to have remained on good terms with the Cassatts. He remained with the firm until 1928 when, aged fifty, he retired to devote himself to gentlemanly pursuits—polo, racquets, golf and, of course, fox hunting. His hunting pack, Mr. Stewart's Cheshire Foxhounds, was recognized in 1914.

Fox hunting hasn't been called the "sport of kings" for nothing. Like this 1920s master of foxhounds, who represented royalty, to the hounds, who played the parts of common soldiers, the sport is reminiscent of medieval warfare. *Cynthia P. Dixon.*

Stewart also remarried, to Carol Averell Harriman Smith, daughter of E.H. Harriman, president of the Union Pacific Railroad. Her brother, Averell Harriman (1891–1986), was Franklin Roosevelt's ambassador to the Soviet Union and adviser to subsequent presidents.

Among Stewart's passions was punctuality. Dinner was served at seven o'clock, not a minute before or earlier, and was always formal. According to his stepdaughter, Nancy Stewart Hannum, two footmen in black trousers and tan dinner coats always served the meal, and stood while the family ate.

"There was only one way to handle the day's important moments—Plunket's way," said Hannum. "One evening, Spence [the butler] announced dinner two minutes early; an appalled Plunket said he would be in the dining room at seven."

On the field, Stewart was a "dictator" who insisted that ladies all ride sidesaddle and forbade liquor. (Flasks became common after his death.) He expected those who were out with his hounds to be well dressed and courteous. Stewart also demanded that hunters stay off tilled ground, not disturb livestock, replace any rails or fences knocked down and close all gates.

As in medieval England, this lifestyle required servants, as well as a certain attitude about servants. Stewart's attitude was that servants were "family," so he resisted when Carol proposed a raise for the stud groom. All of the servants were equally dedicated, he maintained; giving a raise to one would cause "a commotion." (The "family" idea went only so far; after endowing his children during his life, Stewart left his estate—valued only at "over $200,000," the top category in the probate office—to two stepchildren. Eight employees each received about $1,200.)

It seems natural that Plunket Stewart would have been attracted to fox hunting.

Fox hunting is inherently aristocratic, but not merely because it is expensive to play. Its basic form was set on the medieval battlefield, where kings rode surrounded by nobles and often led their troops in person. Replace the armor with tailored red jackets and the common foot soldiers with hounds, and what have you got? A "field" of mounted riders led by a master of the hunt who, assisted by various officials, directs the hounds in their pursuit.

As in medieval warfare, the goal isn't to fight but to win. Large-scale battles were a risk to leaders who preferred to tire an enemy with strategic concentrations of troops. Eventually, losers would "go to ground" in a castle (read: foxhole), where they were dug out with a siege (read: shovel). In either case, the quarry might be killed or, magnanimously, spared. More important than killing was attaining the power of life and death—the ultimate expression of social hierarchy.

For this very reason, hunting has been under attack since the Enlightenment, when middle-class intellectuals first began to consider animals capable of happiness and suffering and therefore feel guilt over the suffering inflicted on them. In 1800, William Wordsworth (1770–1850) published a poem, "Hart's Leap Well," that described the pursuit of a male deer by a yelling crowd of men and dogs. Stag hunting, then considered the most glamorous form of hunting, ended when the animal was torn to death or, if it took to water, when hunters in rowboats slit its throat.

Wordsworth's contemporary, radical English poet (and vegetarian) Percy Bysshe Shelley (1792–1822), railed at Parliament for protecting this "barbarous and bloody sport, from which every enlightened and amiable mind shrinks in abhorrence and disgust."

Hunting's defenders countered that the sport helped educate a military aristocracy. In Parliament, William Windham (1750–1810) insisted that limiting hunting would end the ascendancy of British armies and navies. In *Don Quixote*, when Sancho Panza resists harming a "poor beast," his companion says, "You are mistaken, Sancho. Hunting wild beasts is the most proper exercise for knights and princes; for in the chase of a stout noble beast may be represented the whole art of war." Even today, Charles Coulombe, a U.S. delegate to the International Monarchist League, notes approvingly that the gentry's hunting rules—not shooting a "sitting duck," for instance—are responsible for "much of what we call gentlemanly behavior."

The issue has not died either. Fox hunting was banned in Great Britain in 2005, although Tony Blair, the former prime minister, later said that he hadn't fully understood the issue and regretted promoting the legislation.

One thing is sure: If the purpose of fox hunting were to exterminate a pest, nobody would bother. In England, most foxes killed (57 percent) are simply shot by farmers, according to the British Association of Shooting and Conservation. Another 30 percent are caught in traps. Of the remaining 13 percent, only a fraction is killed by fox hunters. In the United States, foxes are usually spared—both to avoid charges of animal cruelty and because they are often scarce.

Something else is going on: land. Chasing foxes requires a lot of unfenced land so riders can pursue prey wherever it goes. Inevitably, that leads to conflict between fox hunters and farmers trying to grow crops and confine livestock. The issue has existed for a thousand years, since medieval kings claimed all hunting rights, on their own land *and* on everyone else's. Significantly, the right of any citizen to hunt was among those won in the French Revolution.

Locally, in 1853, fox hunter Joseph Worth of West Chester sued an East Bradford farmer, Isaac Darlington, after the latter shot and killed Worth's hound that had entered his property during a hunt. (The judge found for Worth.) In 1858, Mrs. A.G. Cope of Franklin Township, Chester County, complained loudly after cantering fox hunters on a public road spooked the mules pulling her cart home from West Chester.

"When near entering Seeds' Bridge," she wrote to the *Village Republican*, "three of the company passed me at a rapid rate, and I being unable to restrain the mules, followed at the same gait." The mules stampeded across the bridge, the wagon missed a turn and a wheel collapsed. Mrs. Cope wasn't injured but, according to the newspaper, was "greatly alarmed and was quite used up for several days." To their credit, the fox hunters later paid for the damages out of their contingency fund.

As recently as 1984, some fox hunters still seemed determined that nothing interfere with a sport of kings. "A lot of hunters will just go right through your property," Ken Hartung, manager of Crow's Nest Farm in north-central Chester County, told the *Philadelphia Inquirer*. "Now, understand, there are some fine fox hunters. But some of them are awful sneaky. They'll go out on a Sunday morning when they figure you're in church and go right through your property."

This was essentially the situation as Stewart found it. He was "awed by the matchless beauty of southeastern Chester County," said Hannum. But his fox hunting friends scoffed at the idea of turning the myriad "birdcage" (fenced) farms into good fox hunting country.

But what to do about all of those farmers and their fences?

According to Hannum, Stewart solved the problem in one day with a suitcase full of cash. He simply drove down the road, stopping at one farmhouse after another.

"Only Plunket would have thought to call at the farms he wanted to buy all on one day when the farmers wouldn't be in contact with one another," she recalled. "This was before telephones were standard equipment."

For an elderly farmer, the offer was surely attractive: cash on the kitchen table and lifetime tenancy. But Stewart allowed no dawdling. An owner's only decision was to take it or leave it. Immediately.

"Many took it," said Hannum, acknowledging that there were holdouts. "You can look at an old tax map and see exactly which farmers preferred shaky independence to Plunket's brand of financial security."

Stewart didn't keep all of the farms he bought. Some were sold to fellow fox hunters, who used the old farmhouses—which they termed "hunting boxes"—for weekend getaways. Many were vastly expanded to become country estates. The fences, however, all came down. No property was sold to active farmers.

"Plunket worked to create unanimity," said Hannum. "He wanted people to move in who liked open spaces and enjoyed having the hunt ride through their property." Rich people, in other words.

The result was magnificent. In 1941, Stewart and his estate received international notice when he was host to Lord Halifax, the newly appointed British ambassador. Halifax declared that the Stewart hunt—with its miles of rolling green open to anyone with a horse—was just like those in England.

1915

WHEN CHESTER COUNTY STOOD ALONE

B orders are imaginary lines on the ground, but they can mark real differences. That's why politicians can get away with questioning whether states they don't represent are "the real America."

Locally, county borders once indicated positions on women's suffrage. In 1915—five years before passage of the Nineteenth Amendment giving all U.S. women the vote—Chester County was the only county in southeastern Pennsylvania to approve suffrage in a statewide referendum. Of 13,464 votes cast, 55 percent of Chester County voters (all men, of course) voted yes.

In neighboring counties, it wasn't even close. In Delaware County, the prosuffrage vote was 46 percent. And it went down from there: Montgomery County, 40 percent; Philadelphia, 38 percent; Lancaster, 33 percent; and Bucks, 32 percent. The referendum passed in northern and western counties but failed statewide.

Trying to put a good face on it, suffragist leader Katherine Ruschenberger of Strafford naturally pointed out Chester County.

"The Woman Suffrage Party of Chester County desires to thank the men of Chester County for their uniform…kindness shown women at the polls and for placing themselves on record by such a large majority as in favor of justice and fair play," wrote Ruschenberger, the party's secretary for propaganda, two weeks after the election. "The first suffrage meeting was held in Chester County in 1852. The share taken by her men and women in aiding the slave to achieve freedom and justice is well known. It is fitting, therefore, that in this second struggle for justice, Chester County should again lead the eastern counties."

In a 1915 state referendum, supporters used a Liberty Bell replica, the Justice Bell, as a prop for pro-suffrage speakers. The bell was paid for by a woman from Chester County, which was one of the few eastern Pennsylvania counties to approve the measure. *Library of Congress.*

Tradition, politics and demographics made Chester County different. It had a long history of educated and politically active women and strong support for temperance, a movement closely allied with suffrage. In addition, the county was WASPier than most of its neighbors. White Anglo-Saxon Protestants (WASPs) were behind most nineteenth-century social reform movements.

The trend favoring women's suffrage began in Chester County's earliest days. The county was settled by Quakers, who had unique ideas about women. The Delaware River communities, including Philadelphia, were always diverse. But inland Chester County was unsettled territory, and Quakers put their stamp on it.

"The Quaker element," wrote Chester County poet and travel writer Bayard Taylor (1825–1878), "largely predominated in this part of the country; and even the many families who were not actually members of the sect were strongly colored with its peculiar characteristics."

Writing of early nineteenth-century West Chester, historian Douglas Harper put it this way: "What [Quakers] shunned found little light or air in West Chester; their dominance was symbolized by the failure of other churches to take root."

Quakers believed that anyone could know God if divinely inspired. That included women who, as a consequence, had been active socially and in the church since the 1650s. Quaker women traveled in the ministry and, within the church, sometimes had authority over men. All of this virtually mandated that women be educated and made the county receptive to later innovations such as the lyceum movement.

Named for Aristotle's school in Athens, lyceums began in New England in 1826 and spread nationwide. They were created, wrote one historian, to satisfy "hunger for varied knowledge and information" of a population mostly still rural and isolated but nevertheless highly literate. In a time when most Americans had little access to culture, the idea that traveling musicians or speakers might appear at the local schoolhouse was extremely attractive. By 1834, there were more than three thousand lyceums across the United States.

In Tredyffrin Township, the Old Eagle School was Chester County's first lyceum. Others popped up in Dilworthtown, Lionville, Sugartown, Berwyn and Spring City. Most townships had at least one. New Garden Township had three.

Lectures were open to both men and women, and female speakers were not unusual. In 1841, Sarah Fales, a West Chester schoolteacher, gave a six-lecture course in astronomy. Ann Preston (1813–1872) of West Grove, one of the nation's first female physicians, credited her local lyceum with creating the taste for literature that eventually led her to seek higher education. In 1857, Preston herself offered a six-lecture course on "the Laws of Life and the means of Preserving Health."

Science, literature and morality were the main topics. Politics came later, though perhaps not much later in West Chester, where the lyceum early offered a debate on immigration: "Should the term of residence required by the naturalization laws be extended?"

"Among the middle class, especially among young adults," wrote county historians William R. Meltzer and Laurie A. Rofini, "these organizations were a springboard for discussing philosophical, religious and social issues." The men who attended were of the same demographic most likely to vote for it: white, middle class, native born and Protestant. Discussions usually favored women's suffrage.

Formal education was not neglected. The West Chester Boarding School for Girls, established in 1829, offered a high school–level education in the full spectrum of academic subjects, plus needlework, for seventy dollars per term. Harper estimated that 1,200 young women passed through the school during its twenty-two-year history. Affluent families also had a choice of other, smaller private schools. Public schools were opened in 1834 for both boys and girls.

West Chester's location may have attracted organizers of the 1852 convention. A solid base of support existed in both the county and Philadelphia. But abolitionist meetings in Philadelphia had been attacked by mobs. Chester County was safer.

The event, conducted over two days at Horticultural Hall on North High Street, was a clone of Seneca Falls. Resolutions called for equal treatment of women under the law, the right of women to vote and hold office, access to public education and equal pay for equal work. And it was all thoroughly ridiculed. The editor of the *Jeffersonian* newspaper jeered the men in attendance as "old women in pantaloons" and the women as old maids, amazons and infidels.

The impact was minimal. At most, wrote Harper, the convention "did its part to keep the feeble flame of women's rights alive through the 1850s, until it could grow stronger in later decades."

After the Civil War, the top issue for politically aware women was not suffrage but temperance. As they saw it, the ubiquity of liquor encouraged men to drink away their earnings and abuse or abandon their families. Therefore, liquor was a threat to the family. They had a point: between 1790 and 1830, adult Americans drank an average of seventeen gallons of hard liquor per year.

Since women could not vote, they were powerless to curtail the liquor traffic legally. Naturally, therefore, supporters of temperance became supporters of suffrage.

"The causes of temperance and woman suffrage were linked so closely in the minds of the public that the relationship caused problems for both movements," wrote Meltzer and Rofini. "Those who were hesitant about or disagreed with prohibitionism were often less likely to support woman suffrage." The liquor industry was suffrage's consistent enemy.

In Chester County, the first push to curb consumption came from the evangelical churches, particularly the Methodists. But the movement was colored by anti-immigrant bias. Methodists, for instance, generally opposed all use of alcohol. And they noticed that the county's Irish Catholics not only drank but also did so on Sundays.

Many immigrants never forgot the nativist origins of temperance activists. The WASP busybodies' campaign against alcohol was one of several causes—abolition and suffrage were others—that many immigrants did not welcome. Few cared to be equal with blacks or to change their cultural habits and traditions.

Suffragist Carrie Chapman Catt made no bones about it. "Until the closing years of the struggle," she wrote in 1923, "its leaders and members were women of American birth, education and ideals. A remarkable number were daughters of Revolutionary [War ancestors]." Catt found it galling for such women to beg their rights of blacks and foreigners "with views concerning women molded by European tradition."

In Chester County, though, fewer residents were foreign born—12 percent in 1910—than in neighboring counties. In Montgomery County, 17 percent were foreign born; Delaware County, 22 percent; and Philadelphia, 39 percent. In Bucks County, only about 11 percent were foreign born, but that county—like Lancaster and northern Montgomery—was also home to long-settled Germanic farmers who, like recent immigrants, disliked threats to their cultural traditions.

"Among the Plain People," said one historian, "there was only one sphere for women: 'Kinder, Kich un Karich' [children, kitchen and church]."

In 1915, for the first time, suffragists adopted the tactics of a political campaign. Each local group divided its area by precincts and canvassed voters. Across the state, supporters distributed seeds for yellow flowers so that gardeners could show their support. (Yellow was the official suffrage color.)

Both sides set up headquarters in West Chester—suffragists on North High Street and antis on North Church Street. But the antisuffrage office was staffed by outsiders—Miss L.N. Sloan of Philadelphia and Violetta Morrison of York. "Based upon newspaper coverage and surviving campaign materials, the antisuffragists had a relatively low public profile in West Chester and Chester County," wrote Meltzer and Rofini.

The campaign's symbol was the Justice Bell—a replica of the Liberty Bell with the words "established justice" added to the inscription. The bell was paid for personally by Ruschenberger. But its clapper was chained so that it could not ring—symbolizing, said suffragists, how women's voices were legally silenced.

In June 1915, the bell began a three-month, five-thousand-mile tour of Pennsylvania via flatbed truck. In town after town, the bell served as a prop, attracting crowds who then listened to local suffragists who climbed up to speak beside it. The bell was welcomed home in West Chester on October 30 by a parade of Campfire Girls, women on horseback, schoolchildren, college students and suffrage leaders in decorated automobiles.

Chester County's history justified ending the tour within its borders, said Ruschenberger in a concluding rally on the courthouse steps. "The bell," she said, "comes back to its own home."

1931

Gangster, Racketeer, Marine

Active duty military men seldom talk politics. Once they retire, however, stand back.

In 2006, retired U.S. Army major general Paul Eaton campaigned for the removal of Donald Rumsfeld, calling the secretary of defense "incompetent strategically, operationally and tactically." In 1962, retired U.S. Army major general Edwin Walker—after organizing protests against the desegregation of the University of Mississippi—testified to the U.S. Senate that the Kennedy administration was staffed by "sinister men, anti-American, willing and wanting to sell this country out."

And they were polite, compared to what Major General Smedley Butler (1881–1940) of West Chester said of his era's politicians.

Butler—called the "Fighting Quaker" by his men—was, at the time of his death, the most decorated marine in U.S. history. He was awarded the Medal of Honor twice. But after up-close experience with our elected representatives—who fired him for doing his job and court-martialed him for telling the truth—something clicked into place.

Retiring from the Marine Corps, Butler became an outspoken critic of the politicians' interventionist U.S. foreign policy and a regular speaker on the antiwar circuit. His 1935 book, *War Is a Racket*, nailed what Dwight D. Eisenhower would later call the military-industrial complex:

> *I spent 33 years and four months in active military service and during that period I spent most of my time as a high-class muscle man for Big Business, for Wall Street and the bankers. In short, I was a racketeer, a*

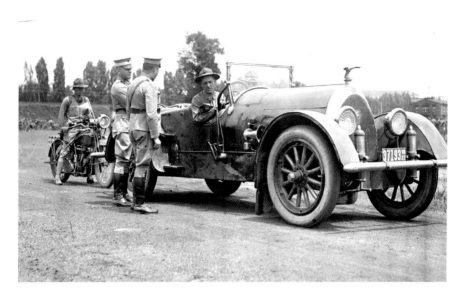

Major General Smedley Butler (seated at the wheel of his car) was the most decorated marine in U.S. history. But up-close experience with his era's politicians led him to reevaluate his own military service and conclude that he had been a "gangster for capitalism." *Library of Congress.*

gangster for capitalism. I helped make Mexico and, especially, Tampico safe for American oil interests in 1914. I helped make Haiti and Cuba a decent place for the National City Bank boys to collect revenues in. I helped in the raping of half a dozen Central American republics for the benefit of Wall Street. I helped purify Nicaragua for the International Banking House of Brown Brothers in 1902–1912. I brought light to the Dominican Republic for the American sugar interests in 1916. I helped make Honduras right for the American fruit companies in 1903. In China in 1927, I helped see to it that Standard Oil went on its way unmolested.

A son of U.S. Representative Thomas S. Butler, Smedley attended West Chester Friends School and then tried to drop out of the Haverford School in 1897 to join the Pennsylvania National Guard. Alerted that he was just sixteen, the Guard sent him home. But when the Spanish-American War broke out the following year, Butler was gone again—this time to the Marine Corps, which made the teen a second lieutenant. Representative Butler insisted that he had pulled no strings. For the rest of his life, the local boy's exploits were a continuing saga in the *Daily Local News.*

The fighting in Cuba was mostly over by the time Butler arrived at his first assignment. Still, a Spanish sniper's near miss allowed him to claim active participation in his first war. A year later, Butler was in the Philippines to fight pro-independence guerrillas who had once fought the Spanish and were now fighting the Americans. In 1900, he arrived in China.

In the nineteenth century, foreign powers had carved up China into spheres of influence in which England, France, Germany, Russia and others claimed exclusive trading rights. The United States had not previously been a part of this. Having recently acquired the nearby Philippines, however, U.S. business interests now wanted in on the action.

The Chinese, meanwhile, wanted the foreigners out. A secret society, Fists of Righteous Harmony, attracted thousands with demands that China free itself of foreign influence. Foreigners called society members "Boxers" because they practiced martial arts. The imperial Qing government quietly encouraged the Boxers, who in early 1900 began killing rural foreign missionaries and their Chinese converts. When the Boxers moved toward the cities, foreign diplomats threw up defenses.

The foreign powers sent in an international relief force to which the United States contributed 2,500 sailors and marines. Among them was Butler, who, while relieving besieged foreigners at Tientsin, was shot in the thigh while rescuing a wounded man. A month later, after a brief recuperation, promotion to captain and a citation for bravery, Butler and his men marched to Beijing, where he was shot in the chest leading his men into the city. A button deflected the bullet. He was just nineteen.

Writing to his father, Butler described desperate Chinese resistance to marines fighting their way into Beijing's culturally important Forbidden City, a district off-limits to all but the royal court. The foreigners used it for a victory parade and to quarter troops and then looted it.

"He is Chester County's hero," editorialized the *Local*, "and when he comes marching home, there will be a royal reception waiting for him." And there was. When Butler came home on leave in December 1900, friends took over the West Chester armory, wrapped it in flags, brought in the Marine Corps band and presented him with a sword.

While Butler had been busy in the Philippines, the United Fruit Company had introduced the banana to Honduras, where landowners adopted it as a cash crop. But Honduras was a country with many have-nots whose frequent revolutions worried United Fruit and other U.S. business interests, which wanted stability. In 1903, Butler and his marines went in to suppress nationalist guerrillas opposing the pro-American government.

With a small force, Butler rescued the U.S. consulate and protected the fruit warehouses and docks.

In 1914, Butler arrived aboard a U.S. warship assigned to protect American citizens and property at Tampico, Mexico, where the U.S. oil industry had immense investments. An unplanned skirmish between U.S. sailors and Mexican soldiers turned into a bombardment and occupation of nearby Veracruz. The incident may have precipitated the fall of President Victoriano Huerta, who was opposed by two rebel groups. Butler won the Medal of Honor.

In 1915, a popular uprising by Haitian nationalists overthrew a pro-American dictator. To protect U.S. business and strategic interests, Woodrow Wilson sent in the marines, who installed a new president and a constitution that, for the first time, allowed foreign ownership of land. The marines—then, as now, with a disproportionate share of southerners in the ranks—further enraged the Haitians by enforcing the Jim Crow rules of the American South as they kept "order" in the streets.

Butler, who led a small force through a culvert to capture a rebel fort, won a second Medal of Honor.

Popular with his men, Butler achieved near sainthood in 1917 at a rainy French debarkation station. With his marines camped in deep mud, he ordered lumber reserved for trenches distributed for four- by six-foot "beds" that would at least allow them to sleep free of the sucking ooze. (Butler personally picked up the first board and carried it for a mile.) Arrested, Butler told superiors that he thought it important to keep the lumber dry, so ordered his marines to protect it with their backs.

Butler's reputation for getting things done was such that, in 1923, it probably seemed like a great idea to have him head the Philadelphia police. Philadelphia was notoriously corrupt and, during the Prohibition era, a major distribution point for liquor. How better to burnish the good-guy image of newly elected mayor, Freeland Kendrick?

So wrong. Nobody could stand next to America's favorite marine and look good.

Butler ordered raids on more than nine hundred speakeasies and went after bootleggers, prostitutes, gamblers and corrupt police. He introduced motorcycle squads and created a signal system to notify beat cops, who had no radios, of fleeing criminals.

Butler apparently spoke in favor of gun confiscation to the *Philadelphia Inquirer*, which in March 1924 used a Butlerian anecdote about how U.S. troops put down the Philippines insurrection: "General Butler…saw many a time the swift value of disarming a hostile foe," noted the paper. "Disarming Philadelphia would prove instantly the greatest check against…highwaymen."

What got Butler in trouble, though, were his raids on upper-crust speakeasies—the Bellevue Stratford and the Union League. Kendrick ordered him to lay off. Butler didn't, and Kendrick fired him. A newspaper quoted Butler as saying, "The people who are running Philadelphia are the rottenest in all hell."

In 1927, Butler and his marines went back China to once again "protect U.S. lives and property." Almost alone, he noticed the growth of Chinese aspirations. "The humblest farmers," he told a reporter, "are fully informed of the Nationalist program."

By now, Butler seems to have applied what he had learned from Philadelphia politicians to the international behavior of national politicians. (After all, they're all politicians, right?) Increasingly, Butler condemned foreign interventions and international saber-rattling. Recalling the Great White Fleet that Theodore Roosevelt sent cruising around the world, Butler observed that other nations were probably as delighted to see foreign warships off their coasts as Americans would be.

"I believe in adequate defense at the coastline and nothing else," said Butler. "The trouble with America is that when the dollar only earns 6 percent over here, then it gets restless and goes overseas to get 100 percent. Then the flag follows the dollar and the soldiers follow the flag."

The end came after a 1931 speech in which Butler discussed how dictators became drunk with power. To illustrate, he repeated a story told him by journalist Cornelius Vanderbilt Jr., who had been riding through the Italian countryside with Benito Mussolini when the dictator hit and killed a child. Mussolini did not even stop. "Never look back in life," he told Vanderbilt, adding that one life was insignificant compared to affairs of state.

Butler's remark that Mussolini was a hit-and-run driver caused an international flap.

In the early 1930s, U.S. officials still admired fascism for its efficiency and support of business interests. Franklin Roosevelt had called Mussolini an "admirable Italian gentleman." In 1934, the U.S. State Department praised a sham Italian election, stating that the fascists' 99 percent victory "demonstrate[d] incontestably the popularity of the Fascist regime."

Arrested and court-martialed, Butler was ordered to apologize. But, at fifty-one, Butler decided that this marine had had enough of saying "yes, sir" to criminals and their defenders. Instead, he retired to a house on Goshen Road near the Aronimink Country Club and began to tell what he knew.

As the marines like to say, "Ooh-rah!"

1945

BY ANY OTHER NAME

Like war, peace is an ideal consumer product. During war, peace is everyone's desire. But once attained, peace eventually becomes dull and tedious. Then we're ready for an exciting new war. It's a self-perpetuating cycle.

This is why, in 1945, Robert Pyle (1877–1951)—a savvy grower and seller of roses who had once publicized a fragrance tour for Helen Keller—chose "Peace" as the trade name of a blossom previously listed as no. 3-35-40. After six years of a war that killed 50 million people, Pyle, president of the Conard-Pyle Company, West Grove, knew that Peace would sell.

Peace remains a national favorite, in part because of the sentimental story that Pyle spread about a grafted bud smuggled out of Europe as France collapsed in 1940 and introduced to America on April 29, 1945, the day Berlin fell.

In fact, Berlin didn't fall until a week later. Perhaps Pyle knew that rose lovers weren't the type to remember that sort of thing.

Born into a Quaker family, Pyle came to the rose business after graduating from Swarthmore College. In 1898, he joined the Conard & Jones Company as secretary, a position he held until 1910.

Conard & Jones was already well established. Founded before the Civil War as a tree nursery by Charles Dingee, the company originally sold a wide variety of shrubs, vines, bulbs, seeds and houseplants. Roses were not originally part of the inventory, but according to several accounts, Dingee added them at his wife's request about 1868. He also took on several partners, including Alfred F. Conard, under whose direction the company distributed the nation's first mail-order rose catalogue.

Rose grower Robert Pyle (right) and Francis Meilland collaborated in the introduction of the beloved Peace rose in 1945. Pyle cooked up a sentimental story about the blossom that, while not strictly true, capitalized on the public's desire for an end to war. *Conard-Pyle Company.*

Roses in that era fell into two broad categories: wild roses—which provided the breeding material—and what gardeners now call old garden roses. Old garden roses are hybrids of wild roses developed in the nineteenth century and before. Typically, they are fragrant, cold hardy and disease resistant. Most bloom only once a year—typically in June—though there are exceptions.

In 1867, rose breeders crossed two old garden varieties—the tea rose (named for the resemblance of its fragrance to that of Chinese black tea) and the repeat-blooming hybrid perpetual—to produce the pale pink "La France." This "hybrid tea rose" became the foundation for an entirely new class of climbers and shrubs now known collectively as modern garden roses.

In the twentieth century, the popularity of hybrid teas eclipsed all others. Gardeners liked their season-long blooms. Flower arrangers liked their large blooms, diverse colors and long, stiff branches. (Older roses often flop on weak stems.) On the down side, hybrid teas don't have much foliage and can be considered ugly in the landscape. Even worse, the blossoms don't have much fragrance, and the plants are more susceptible to disease. None of that mattered. Perhaps hybrid teas appealed to the same Edwardian faith in progress that gave the world air travel, automobiles, bicycles and the *Titanic*.

The Peace rose had a great name for 1945, which saw the end of World War II. But it was also a hybrid tea, which made it extremely high maintenance by modern standards. Increasingly, busy modern gardeners prefer pest- and disease-resistant old garden roses. *Conard-Pyle Company.*

Conard-Pyle—as Pyle renamed the company—followed the trend, and he became a leading advocate for hybrid teas. In *How to Grow Roses*, Pyle's 1906 book that went through twenty editions over forty years, Pyle declared that there was "not a single purpose demanded of the rose which the hybrid tea cannot supply: roses for exhibition, brightening the garden, bedding, pillars, house decoration, buttonholes."

The hybrid teas' maintenance issues stuck him as nothing much. "Sulphur for diseases and arsenate of lead for insects can conveniently be put on together, in a rather simple application," he wrote. "The nicotine preparation [also for insects] is used separately. Thus, no matter what afflictions may threaten the roses, thorough and continuous dusting or spraying with sulphur and arsenate of lead or an approved equivalent will take care of most of them, and nicotine need be used only when necessary."

"Regular and continuous" dusting of hybrid teas, by the way, meant weekly or after each rain. In addition, the plants required regular fertilizer and water (though not too much). For Japanese beetles—common in southeastern Pennsylvania—the prevailing wisdom was to cut flowers each morning before they attacked.

Is it any wonder that hybrid teas' popularity faded in the late twentieth century? Today, pest- and disease-resistant old garden roses have returned to wide popularity.

Pyle's real contribution seems to have been as a businessman and a marketer. In 1910, the company narrowed its focus exclusively to roses. It also became the first to "brand" what had previously been a generic product. Thenceforth, Conard-Pyle roses became Star® roses by Conard-Pyle.

In the 1920s, as a grower and an officer of the national horticultural, rose and other societies, Pyle lobbied Congress for the right to patent plants. The Plant Patent Act of 1930 afforded protection to plants reproduced by "grafting, budding, cuttings, layering, division, and the like, but not by seeds." This allowed Conard-Pyle to collect royalties on its creations, which later brought it a great deal of money.

About 13,000 plant patents have been issued since 1931, but the number surged in the early twenty-first century. Then, about 500 new plant patents were issued each year. Between 1975 and 2005, more than 1,500 patents were granted for new roses.

Pyle excelled at getting media attention. In 1939, he encouraged residential plantings of roses in West Grove and Avondale by offering two free climbing roses to any family that promised to care for them. The *Kennett News & Advertiser* reported that the company gave away about two hundred plants, which were distributed through the schools.

Favored gimmicks included prominent people and current events. In 1939, for instance, Pyle discovered that presenting roses named "Miss Dorothy James" to the daughter of Pennsylvania governor Arthur James at the Philadelphia Flower Show got his company mentioned in all the papers. Quickly, he became more ambitious.

In 1941, when Grand Duchess Charlotte of Luxembourg arrived in the United States as a refugee after German armies rolled through her country, Pyle met her at a New York airport with a large bouquet of "Grand Duchess Charlotte" roses.

"Because the appeal of the rose is universal," he told reporters, "it can also symbolize the sympathy we feel toward Her Highness and her people, now under the heel of the dictator." In 1946, he airmailed an arrangement of "the world's tiniest roses" to Clementine Churchill, then an object of popular sympathy after her husband was defeated for reelection.

In 1951, an army nurse in Korea asked for two Peace roses to plant on the Pusan Perimeter, a small pocket into which Allied troops had been pushed by the invading Chinese. Pyle sent four plants. Later, he distributed to the press copies of the nurse's description of regularly seeing as many as twenty Koreans "just sitting around the bushes, admiring the flowers."

Hybrid tea no. 3-35-40 came to West Grove from French grower Francis Meilland, with whom Conard-Pyle had a testing and marketing alliance. To learn how new roses would perform in various climates, growers usually sent buds to trusted colleagues whose reports determined whether and where the plants would be offered commercially. Meilland, who had been working with no. 3-35-40 since 1935, thought it had promise and sent grafted buds to growers in Germany, Italy and Turkey. Shipping to the West was harder, but a U.S. consul volunteered to carry a small package on the last U.S.-bound aircraft from occupied France. A few days later, Pyle had his rose.

As the war raged, Conard-Pyle propagated additional copies of no. 3-35-40 and sent them to growers around the country. Testing took a couple of growing seasons, but the response was positive. Based on that, Pyle set to work building the company's inventory and scheduled release for the spring of 1945. In Europe, Meilland named the rose "Madame Antoine Meilland" for his mother. The German grower called it "Gloria Dei" (praise be to God) and the Italian "Gioia" (smile).

Ever the promoter, Pyle ran a contest among U.S. rosarians, who chose the name "Peace." Understandably.

After the Germans' December 1944 offensive failed, it was clear to all (except maybe Hitler) that the end of the war was coming. The official debut was scheduled for April 29 at the Pacific Rose Society's spring show in Pasadena. When Pyle told the crowd that "this greatest new rose of our time" had been named for the world's "greatest desire," employees released caged doves.

On that day in Berlin, a just-married Hitler was demanding that his mostly imaginary armies attack the eight Russian armies surrounding the city. Overhead, there was furious fighting around the Reichstag. The next day, Hitler's body was carried outside by aides and incinerated in a crater as bombs continued to fall. On May 1, Hitler's replacement, Admiral Donitz, ordered the "utmost resistance." The Germans' Berlin garrison did not surrender until May 2. The general surrender came on May 8, celebrated as V-E Day.

So, how did Pyle get away with claiming—and generations of garden writers with repeating—that Peace appeared on the day Berlin fell? With chutzpah and marketing and by never looking back. In June, when representatives of forty-five nations gathered in San Francisco to sign the United Nations charter, Pyle paid hotel bellhops one dollar per rose to put a Peace in each delegate's hotel room with a note that read, "We hope the Peace rose will influence men's thoughts for everlasting world peace."

Peace, of course, is a very nice rose. Its pale gold petals and other good (for a hybrid tea) characteristics won the American Rose Society's gold medal in 1946. More than 100 million plants have since been sold.

But what it most had was a great name for the moment and a public that was ready to buy.

BIBLIOGRAPHY

Ashmead, Henry Graham. *History of Delaware County, Pennsylvania.* Philadelphia, PA: L.H. Everts & Co., 1884.

Bacon, Margaret Hope. *The Quiet Rebels: The Story of the Quakers in America.* Wallingford, PA: Pendle Hill Publications, 2000.

Blatt, Martin H., Thomas J. Brown and Donald Yacovone, eds. *Hope & Glory: Essays on the Legacy of the 54th Massachusetts Regiment.* Amherst: University of Massachusetts Press, 2009.

Bombaugh, Charles C., and John B. Lewis. *Strategies and Conspiracies to Defraud Life Insurance Companies.* Baltimore, MD: James H. McClellan Publisher, 1896.

Darlington, William. "Address of Wm. Darlington, M.D., L.L.D." *American Republican*, October 24, 1854.

Faust, Drew Gilpin. *This Republic of Suffering: Death and the American Civil War.* New York: Random House, 2008.

Harper, Douglas R. *West Chester to 1865: That Elegant & Notorious Place.* West Chester, PA: Chester County Historical Society, 1999.

Hole, Helen. *Westtown Through the Years.* Westtown, PA: Westtown Alumni Association, 1942.

Hunter, William E. *Edward Hunter, Faithful Steward.* Salt Lake City, UT: Publishers Press, 1970.

Katzenstein, Caroline. *Lifting the Curtain: The State and National Woman Suffrage Campaign in Pennsylvania as I Saw Them.* Pittsburgh: Dorrance & Co., 1955.

McFarland, J. Horace, and Robert Pyle. *How to Grow Roses.* New York: Macmillan Company, 1945.

Meltzer, William R., and Laurie Rofini. "The Woman Suffrage Campaign in West Chester." *West Chester, the First 200 Years: 1799–1999*, 1999. West Chester, PA: Taggart Printing Corp., 1999.

Mohr, Nancy L. *The Lady Blows a Horn*. Warrenton, VA: Horse Country Press, 1997.

Nuermberger, Ruth K. *The Free Produce Movement: A Quaker Protest Against Slavery*. Brooklyn, NY: AMS Press, 1970.

Peitzman, Stephen J. *A New and Untried Course: Women's Medical College and Medical College of Pennsylvania, 1850–1998*. Camden, NJ: Rutgers University Press, 2000.

Preston, Ann. *Cousin Ann's Stories for Children*. San Francisco, CA: Inner Light Books, 2010.

Price, Isaiah, DDS. *History of the Ninety-Seventh Regiment, Pennsylvania Volunteer Infantry, During the War of the Rebellion, 1861–65*. Philadelphia, PA: Isaiah Price, 1875.

Sellers, Charles Coleman. *Theophilus the Battle-Axe: A History of the Lives and Adventures of Theophilus Ransom Gates and the Battle-Axes*. Philadelphia, PA: Patterson & White Company, 1930.

Smedley, R.C. *History of the Underground Railroad in Chester and the Neighboring Counties of Pennsylvania*. Mechanicsburg, PA: Stackpole Books, 2005.

Smith, John. "A Narrative of Some Sufferings for His Christian Peaceable Testimony, by John Smith, late of Chester County, deceased." *The Friend: A Religious and Literary Journal* (Tenth Month 22, 1887).

Stephens, George E. *Voice of Thunder*. Champaign: University of Illinois Press, 1997.

Taylor, George W. *Autobiography and Writings of George W. Taylor*. Philadelphia, PA: self-published, 1891.

Underhill, Paco. *Why We Buy: The Science of Shopping*. New York: Simon & Schuster, 1999.

Walker, Peter F. *Moral Choices: Memory, Desire and Imagination in Nineteenth-Century American Abolition*. Baton Rouge: Louisiana State University Press, 1979.

Wells, Susan. *Out of the Dead House: 19th Century Women Physicians and the Writing of Medicine*. Madison: University of Wisconsin Press, 2001.

ABOUT THE AUTHOR

Mark E. Dixon has lived in the Delaware Valley since 1987, when he moved from Texas to a Drexel Hill apartment complex where *American Bandstand*'s Dick Clark once lived. Though not himself a native, he grew up hearing about "the beautiful city of Philadelphia" from his mother, who had moved here in 1945 to do social work and ended up marrying a Hahnemann University medical student from Michigan. And the roots go deeper: Dixon's mother's chose Philadelphia based on stories told by *her* grandmother. In 1886, Dixon's great-grandmother—a descendant of some of the region's earliest settlers—was a shopgirl at Wanamaker's Grand Court, opposite City Hall in Philadelphia. And there, though it was surely against John Wanamaker's rules, great-grandmother let herself be romanced by—and later married—a Midwestern Quaker who was in town on business but needed a pair of gloves. Those tales provided a window into the area's history, later expanded by Dixon's joining the Religious Society of Friends (Quakers), which is practically a historical society itself.

The public relations job that drew Dixon to the area vanished in a spectacular corporate bankruptcy three years later. Eventually, he returned to work as a writer—this time freelance—building on earlier experience as a reporter for newspapers and trade publications. The stories in this book are columns that he began writing for *Main Line Today* magazine in 2003. Dixon and his family live in Wayne.